"This is an honest and e... a mum with primary school-going children. ... in one sitting because the book had me laughing out loud at so many points. It was as funny as it was touching. I enjoyed it thoroughly because I could see myself and my kids behaving in the exact same way."

—Jane Ng, Correspondent, *The Sunday Times*

"This book should carry a warning: do not read where you cannot collapse in giggles! It is a hilarious first-hand account of competitive parenting in Singapore, full of laugh-out-loud moments; and animated by a mixture of exasperation, self-flagellation and tenderness that will resonate with parents, teachers and all who love and care for children. A delicious, delightful read."

—Tisa Ho (Ng), Executive Director, Hong Kong Arts Festival and Board Member, Hong Kong International Literary Festival

"Quintessential Singapore experience told with humour, candour and no compunction. A delightful read, especially at night. You will go to bed knowing you are not alone."

—Diana Ser, Managing Director, Diana Ser Communications

THE GOOD, THE BAD
AND THE
THE PSLE

Trials of an Almost
Kiasu Mother

MONICA LIM

EPIGRAM BOOKS / SINGAPORE

Cover design by Stefany
Edited by Ruth Wan and Sheri Tan

Published with the support of

NATIONAL ARTS COUNCIL
SINGAPORE

National Library Board, Singapore
Cataloguing-in-Publication Data

Lim, Monica.

The good, the bad and the PSLE :
trials of an almost kiasu mother / by Monica Lim.
– Singapore : Epigram Books, 2013.
pages cm

ISBN : 978-981-07-6599-6 (paperback)
ISBN: 978-981-07-6600-9 (ebook)

Motherhood – Fiction. I. Title.

PZ7
S823 -- dc23   OCN840850238

This is a work of fiction. Names, characters, places, and incidents either are the product
of the author's imagination or are used fictitiously. Any resemblance to actual persons,
living or dead, events, or locales is entirely coincidental.

First Edition

10 9 8 7 6 5 4 3 2 1

For my writing buddy,
my muse and my facilitator.
You know who you are
and I love you all
very much.

CONTENTS

YEAR

1

TERM 1

Prelude

I can't believe my baby is going to Primary One. As I helped Noah pack his school bag for the next day, I had a feeling of déjà vu. Didn't I just help him pack his bag for his first day of preschool? Seems like it was only yesterday.

Actually, he hasn't changed all that much. He's just a little taller, somewhat tougher and a whole lot rounder. I really need to break his fried food addiction.

I placed his pencil case, 1A textbooks and a couple of exercise books into his bag. That seemed like the bare minimum but the bag was already surprisingly heavy.

Then I remembered the water bottle, packet of tissue, file, notebook and school diary, by which time the Ben 10 bag looked bulkier than Noah and probably weighed as much. Maybe I should have bought him a trolley bag.

I mused out loud. "I wonder who your teacher will be."

"Remember to find out how to go to the toilet."

"Jie Jie got into the best Primary Four class. Isn't your big sister clever? I wonder which class you'll be in."

"Isn't this exciting?"

When I turned around from my monologue, I realised that Noah had been playing with his toy cars the whole time, not having heard a word I said. Big sister April was standing in the corner of the room, looking amused.

"Mummy, I think you're more thrilled about primary school than he is," she said.

"The first day of school is exciting!" I protested. "Noah, if you have any worries or questions about the school, just ask Jie Jie, okay? She can help you. She knows the place inside out. Is there anything you would like to know? About the teachers? The classrooms? The subjects?"

Noah looked up at April expectantly. "Does the canteen sell fried chicken?"

Square One

I am so thankful Noah has gotten a place in Somerset Primary School on account of having an older sibling there.

April's teacher told me the school has become so popular that you now need to ballot during the Primary One registration exercise to get a place. Just because the school produced the top Primary School Leaving Examination (PSLE) student two years ago. Singaporeans are so kiasu! If there was an exam that measured our fear of losing out, I'm sure we'd score top marks as a nation.

It is reassuring to know the school can produce good results for the Primary Six national exams though. Even though Papa feels otherwise, academic results are very important in order to do well in Singapore. Hopefully, the environment at Somerset Primary School will nurture Noah's interest in studying.

Noah will be taking the school bus to and from school, but just for today I took leave to drive him on this momentous occasion. I would have preferred it if he could have gone to school with April but this is one of those rare schools which still has morning and afternoon sessions. Primary Ones and Twos are in the afternoon session, the rest are in the morning.

Noah scrunched up his face when putting on his school uniform as the white shirt was still starchy in its newness. Mental note: use more softener. He did look smart in it, though. My baby's all grown up!

We arrived at school half an hour early. I wanted to be sure I could get a parking lot and my foresight paid off. The students were supposed to assemble at the canteen, so

I took Noah there and made sure he joined the line for the right class. Pretty soon, the canteen started to fill up as kids straggled in.

One girl stood in the middle of the courtyard with a florid pink Hello Kitty school bag, looking dazed. A teacher tried asking the girl her name and class but she remained unresponsive. A parent watching the situation nearby remarked, "No ring tone."

In contrast, a couple of worldly-wise girls were already chatting with each other like they were the best of friends, comparing how much pocket money they had. I was sure the loser would use the information as a bargaining tool with her parents later.

Amid the chaos, order ensued. Experienced teachers, veterans of many first days of school, established queues of twos and led the children to their classrooms. I followed Noah to his, where he found a seat. There he was, in his crisp, oversized uniform, still clutching his Ben 10 school bag, looking slightly lost. His sister was so different. By the end of the first day of Primary One, she had been appointed class monitor and had helped the teacher hand out books. She even pretended not to see me when I waved at her through the classroom window, making me look like one of those silly eager beaver mums.

Noah, on the other hand, brightened when he saw me standing outside his classroom and kept waving enthusi-astically. After a while, I realised that the distraction had caused him to miss what his teacher had been saying for the last 30 minutes, so I beat a hasty retreat to the canteen.

I waited till it was time for recess and after scanning the sea of white uniforms that had streamed into the canteen, spotted Noah with his Primary Two buddy. They sat on a bench eating their snacks. After I saw the mob around the stalls, I was glad I had made Noah bring a lunchbox. The queues were held up by some trigger-happy parents who kept pointing their cameras at their clearly bewildered newbies, instructing, "Smile, darling! Hold up the chicken rice!"

Oh, the digital age, where we have to document every single moment of our lives! Actually, I brought a camera too but at least I only took photos of Noah getting out of the car, at assembly and in the classroom.

After recess had ended, I decided to spend the rest of the school day waiting in the canteen and used the time to reply to some emails from my editor. Thank goodness I had the presence of mind to bring my laptop. Not for the first time, I felt a deep sense of gratitude for being able to enjoy a flexible work arrangement, so I could juggle work and time with my kids. I had worked as a full-time journalist at *Realities*, a lifestyle magazine, for 10 years covering the travel beat, before I discovered that I was pregnant with April. Having read about the problems of latchkey kids, I was determined not to be an absentee parent and switched to a part-time position. My editor was fully supportive and gave me a pretty long leash, as long as I handed in my articles on time. It was a near-perfect arrangement.

I managed to clear quite a bit of administrative work by 6.15pm, when the students came streaming out of their classrooms like swarms of ants. I walked towards the car park where I had told Noah to meet me. Soon enough, he appeared, dragging his school bag behind him. I knew it was too heavy.

"So how was your first day?" I asked as we got into the car.

"Okay."

"What else?" I prodded as I started the car, impatient for more details. "Was your teacher nice? What did you do?"

Long pause. "I couldn't find my class."

I gripped the steering wheel. "What do you mean you couldn't find your class? I saw you there!"

"After recess, my buddy brought me to the toilet. When I came out, he was gone."

"Oh dear! What did you do then?"

"I stood at the staircase and cried until a teacher found me."

Misadventure on the first day of school! That didn't bode well. Trying to salvage the situation, I tried another tack.

"Did you make friends? I'm sure you made friends. Who's your partner?"

"Her name is Summer. I don't like her."

"Why?"

"She kept pressing the light switch on my watch."

Doh.

Common Cents

In December, before the school year started, Somerset Primary organised an orientation programme for children about to enter Primary One, as well as their parents. At the parents' session, the Principal told us to teach our kids how to count money, so they could buy food at the canteen. I found it odd that counting money was in the Primary One Maths syllabus, yet the kids were expected to have mastered this skill before they started school.

Dutifully, I tried to teach Noah, but it was harder than I thought. The dollars were easy but cents were confusing. It also took him a long time to apply the concept of 100 cents = $1. When you'd only just learnt how to count to 100 and to mentally add single digits, working out change from up to $2 was very complicated.

"If the chicken rice costs $1.25 and you give the auntie $2, how much change should she return you?"

Noah said slowly, "Wait, that means 200 minus 125…" He was deep in thought for a while. Finally he exclaimed, "I can't do it in my head! Give me a piece of paper. I have to write it down."

I didn't think the tuck shop auntie would have that much patience.

A few sessions of playing shop with disastrous change-giving later, I gave up. In the end, it was the worldly-wise older sister who came up with a food-buying tip. "No need to know how much change you'll get," April told Noah.

"Just give the auntie a $2 note. She'll give you back the right change."

After the first day of school, Noah declared that he wanted to buy his own food so I gave him pocket money and hoped he would be able to manage well enough not to go hungry. On the second day of school, relishing his new-found freedom, he marched up to the ice cream stall and told the stall keeper, "I want the colourful ice cream."

Within the first week, he had bought French fries, crackers and nuggets, all the food I frown upon. He even managed to buy a can of 100Plus from the vending machine. That was an accident though. He bought it because it was the only available drink in a can and he thought it would be like Coca-Cola, which was forbidden fruit to him. He was so short he had to enlist his buddy's help to put the coins in the machine for him. I laughed mercilessly at him when he told me it tasted funny.

My conclusion is: if your kid is a greedy gut, nothing will stop him from getting his snacks. Not being able to count money is but a minor inconvenience.

First Impressions

Noah has not taken to his form teacher, Miss Wee, which is a pity. Here is a boy who hates seatwork and has the attention span of a gnat. I was hoping he would get a fantastic, fun-loving teacher who could inspire him and encourage him to take an interest in his studies.

No such luck. I've already gotten a note from her, gently asking if I could tell Noah to focus more in class. It doesn't look good for the rest of the year.

His biggest pet peeve with her is that she is strict about talking in class. I can see how this would be a huge turn-off for Mr Personality. Asking him not to chat with a friend is like asking him not to breathe. Plus, I imagine talking helps him pass the time when he's bored in class. For Noah, school is about friends and fun. Studies are merely a diversion.

I tried pleading with him. "I never got a single note from Jie Jie's teacher in all her three years! It's not even been two months and I'm getting a note from your teacher. Can you at least try harder to concentrate?"

He looked contrite but I know his flesh is weak. It doesn't help that his memory is not a sponge but a sieve (it retains only the useless bits). When he gets dropped off by the school bus at home every day, I would greet him at the door and ask, "How was school?"

His usual reply: "Okay."

"What did you do?"

He would look stumped as if I'd just asked him to recite the 12 times table. Finally he would give me an irrelevant fact like, "Summer was not feeling well. She vomited in class."

I still recall after his school orientation before his entry into Primary One, I asked him what he had learnt. He thought about it for a while and said, "I cannot bring pets to school like spiders." That was all he could remember of the entire four-hour orientation programme.

The bright side about being Mr Personality is that he has already made lots of friends. His best buddy is Ming Hao and the two of them regularly run off to play soccer with a whole bunch of other boys during recess. When I asked Noah what Ming Hao was like, he replied, "Fat and funny. And he likes potato chips."

Two peas in a pod.

Hello, Goodbye

Sometimes I marvel at how one set of parents can produce such different children. April is a thinker and planner. She is smart and strives to do well in school. Noah is clueless, hyperactive and lives for the moment.

Their contrasting personalities mean fights are almost inevitable. There are two phrases that I've grown thoroughly sick of hearing: "It's not fair!" and "It's not my fault!" When I can't stand it anymore, I would just confiscate whatever they're fighting over. Nobody wins and then they get to commiserate over a common enemy: mean old Mummy.

It's not just over belongings that they quarrel about. When they were younger, it was over things like who got to press the lift button, who got to use the bathroom first, who got to hold my right hand (what's wrong with the left one?)

Once, after overhearing another meaningless round of bickering, I said in exasperation, "You two are like a cat and a dog!"

Noah perked up. "Who's the dog?" he asked.

April: "I want to be the dog."

Noah: "HAHHH, not fair! I want to be the dooooooog!"

(Several rounds of "I'm the dog!" and "No, I'm the dog!")

April (finally): "Okay, then I'm the cat and I will SCRATCH you!"

Noah: "MUUMMMMYYYYYYYYY!!!!!!"

Having said that, I suspect that deep down, they are fond of each other in their own way. Even though April thinks her brother is a nuisance, I have seen her defend him when he was being bullied at the playground.

Noah, despite his insistence that all girls are annoying, secretly admires his sister for having skills like knowing how to make a Lego house and sewing a busted seam on his teddy. In fact, until recently, he thought he was going to marry April when he grew up. When I told him he couldn't marry his sister, he protested, "But Grandma said 'next time when you two get married'…"

"She didn't mean to each other lah!" Haiz…

You should have seen April's expression. I'm sure she was thinking, who in their right mind would want to marry Noah?

I have a dream that one day the two of them will be the best of friends. I hope this is not one of those pipe dreams.

学华语 (or "How to Learn the World's Most Complicated Language")

April has had Chinese tuition since she was in Primary Two and I started Noah on it a few weeks ago, much to his chagrin. I didn't have a choice; his Chinese is atrocious. Since Papa and I are not particularly fluent in Mandarin ourselves, we couldn't provide our children with a good foundation in the language when they were younger, so they grew up with little exposure to it.

When Noah was in preschool, he had problems understanding what the Chinese teacher was saying. Rather than clarify his doubts however, he channelled his survival skills and simply nodded intelligently to everything she said. The truth finally dawned on her and she told me, "Mrs Tan, Noah has been copying his friend's work."

"How can you be sure that he copied the work?" I asked a little defensively.

"Because he even copied his friend's name."

Noah's Chinese hasn't improved much since then. He can barely recognise basic words and he speaks Mandarin like an ang moh. In fact, I'm sure a Caucasian would get more tones right than Noah. His intonation is seemingly random even for the simplest words and phrases.

For instance, instead of "吃鱼" (eat fish), he would say "吃雨" (eat rain). "喝水" (drink water) becomes "河水" (river water) and "飞机" (aeroplane) becomes "肥鸡" (fat chicken). I make both kids watch the Chinese TV drama

书包太重 but Noah habitually says "树包" instead of "书包" (school bag), prompting me to ask, "What? You carry a tree bag?"

When he writes his Chinese characters, it's as if the squares in the exercise book don't exist. They are there for decorative purposes only. His words flow languidly across the borders, encroaching on other characters' spaces.

Noah scored only 7/10 for his first two 听写, which I told him was unacceptable for Primary One. A parent's signature was required for all Chinese spelling exercises so I threatened, "If you don't get 10/10, I won't sign your book." After a while, I realised that he had not let me sign his 听写 book for a couple of weeks. When I asked him about it, he replied matter-of-factly, "You said if I don't get 10/10, you won't sign my book so I signed it myself."

Needless to say, I went into a lengthy sermon on how forging your parent's signature was one deep, dark step into a moral abyss.

The Chinese tutor is a very patient lady but I sometimes hear an edge creep into her voice. It's hard to motivate someone who has zero interest in the subject. During lessons, I've seen Noah place his head on the table like he's totally weary or stare gloomily at his book. I've also overheard him trying to negotiate with the tutor, "So much work! I can't do it. Can I do half?"

Last week, he told me that his legs sometimes hurt.

"When?" I asked, concerned, wondering if he had injured himself playing soccer.

"When I sit down during tuition."

Privately, I feel sorry for him. I know how difficult it is for children from English-speaking households to learn Chinese. Even April, who is so hardworking, finds it tough going sometimes. The Chinese tutor makes her memorise lists of good phrases so that she can do well in her Chinese composition and so far, this has worked. Never mind that it is not the most creative or original way to write a composition. Based on how compositions are marked, it is the easiest way to score points.

"Chinese is so difficult," April lamented, as she prepared to memorise the latest list of 好词好句 given by the Chinese tutor.

But we don't have a choice, right? The government says we have to be bilingual and if you're Chinese, you need to learn Mandarin. And from what I hear, if you're bad at it, it's going to completely pull down your PSLE score. I have to make sure both of them keep up or I'll have bigger problems later on.

This Used to Be My Playground

Every fortnight, I take April and Noah to the library. This is April's playground. For her, every book is an adventure, a passage into the unknown, something to be discovered. She devours books with an insatiable appetite. Her quota of six books on her library card is never sufficient so she always asks to borrow my card.

I'm gratified to see that her level of reading has been steadily rising. All the children's classics that I recommended to her—*Charlotte's Web*, *The Secret Garden*, *The Wizard of Oz* —she finished during the December holidays. One afternoon, I saw her wholly absorbed in *Animal Farm* and was amazed by how advanced she was. At this rate, her command of the language is sure to improve exponentially.

In this respect, April is exactly like me when I was young. I practically camped out at the library when I was growing up and even bought exercise books to copy out passages from my favourite library books. I guess it's no surprise that I became a journalist.

The library is also Noah's playground but in a more literal sense. Take today, for instance. After I had told him to pick six books, he wandered around listlessly before coming back with six picture books! Three were on fire engines, one was a Dr Seuss book and the other two were *Tintin* comics.

I told him he wasn't a baby anymore and tried showing him Beverly Cleary's *Henry Huggins*. He wrinkled his nose and said it looked boring, so I went off to search for more options. When I returned with an armful of books, Noah wasn't where he was supposed to be. Looking around, I spotted him weaving in and out of the bookshelves in the Adult Fiction section, hiding behind chairs, aiming an imaginary pistol at covert villains and dodging invisible bullets.

Ohhhhhh! This boy will be the death of me. As I muttered, "God, give me strength," and took a step towards him, the inevitable happened. Noah's fantasy came to an abrupt end as he crashed into a librarian's cart and a shower of books fell on the ground. A commotion followed, whereby the librarian made disapproving noises and told him off reproachfully. Several library users looked up from their books and stared at me. I know when I'm being judged.

I hurried over, whispered hasty apologies to the librarian and grabbed Noah's arm. Together with April, we left in a flurry. All the way to the car park, I berated Noah on the importance of behaving well in public and not being an embarrassment to his longsuffering mother. It was only when we were about to get into the car that April exclaimed, "Mummy, we forgot the books!"

I'll just have to find another library where I can show my face.

TERM 2

The Homework Battle

Getting Noah to finish his homework has become a daily chore. Almost every day, I have to nag at him to finish his worksheets and this inevitably degenerates into a battle of wills.

Prying him off the couch and away from Cartoon Network takes 15 minutes. When he has finally found his worksheet among the unsorted and ever-growing pile of paper in his bag, another 10 minutes would have passed. After he settles down at his desk, I can expect that within 10 minutes, he would inexplicably need to use the bathroom. Throughout the entire torturous process, he would need to drink water, sharpen his pencil, find his eraser, cut his nails and use the bathroom again. Repeat cycle.

It's clockwork.

Surely it's too early for me to feel jaded? This is just Term Two of Primary One! I'm tired of hearing myself yell. It's not an attractive sound even to my own ears.

I guess I should have seen it coming. Even in preschool, Noah had a natural aversion to anything he deemed as 'work'. We're not talking rocket science, we're talking about something as simple as colouring. He would carefully lay out the picture he had to colour on his desk, and take 10 minutes to do all the peripheral activities like turning on the light and looking for his coloured pencils.

Then he would take another 10 minutes to arrange his coloured pencils and choose a colour (apparently a very complicated thought process). Blue?…Or red?…Decisions, decisions. Finally when he was ready to start, he would proceed to conscientiously colour a corner of the picture… for about five minutes, before heaving a huge sigh and declaring that he was "so tired".

Whenever I have to fill in a form asking about Noah's allergies, I'm tempted to write 'homework'.

Today was especially exasperating. I needed him to finish his Maths worksheet quickly so that he could move on to his Chinese tuition homework. I sat him down, made sure he had his pencil, eraser, ruler and water (I didn't want him making excuses about needing to fill his water bottle). I even made him go to the bathroom first.

Half an hour later, when I checked on his progress, I discovered to my horror that he had only written his name! He had been playing with his eraser the whole time. After I had released a torrent of loud threats, Noah turned to me with tears in his eyes and said sadly, "Even though you scold me, Mummy, I still love you."

Great. Now I have guilt.

Joyride

I have never understood the male obsession with cars. Before I had a son, I couldn't figure out why toy stores sold a gazillion different types of miniature vehicles. I mean, a toy car is a toy car, right? Boy, was I off the mark and on a whole different planet. Apparently, every boy needs the entire collection of convertibles, sedans, four-wheel drives, diggers, trucks, vans, buses and taxis, and in EVERY SINGLE COLOUR. I would name more except I'm hindered by my limited transportation vocabulary. At the height of his craze, Noah had almost 200 little vehicles and he still complained he didn't have "the Hong Kong taxi in blue".

I also found out that the male species never outgrows this phase—the cars just get bigger. Papa loves his 12-year-old Alfa Romeo passionately, even though it's as temperamental as a teenage girl on a candy diet. It would break down petulantly at the most inopportune moments, like on the expressway during peak hour traffic or when

I'm rushing to fetch the kids.

To me, the Alfa is more trouble than it's worth. I'd much rather own a reliable, nondescript Japanese sedan that serves its purpose of actually working as a mode of transportation. But then, I'm no petrol head like Papa. "Ling, the Alfa has personality," he would say.

Right. Personality shouldn't need to function on premium parts that are regularly out of stock and ridiculously hard to come by, as if they're handcrafted by indigenous tribesmen on a remote island.

The trouble is, I'm the one who has to drive the car most of the time, since Papa works downtown and his office is conveniently located next to an MRT train station. So even though I'm a nervous driver, I accept that with my flexible work schedule, I have to be the one driving the kids for CCAs and other school activities.

There have been a few near misses and once, a concrete side wall eluded my eyes and multiple mirrors when I was parking. Papa was rather miffed that I had dented his beloved. Then it was his turn. Recently, he got into a fender bender and when he called to inform me of the unfortunate incident, my first thought, shamefully, was not: "Was anybody hurt?" but: "Lucky not me."

I'm one of those drivers who would proceed at a snail's pace when filtering onto a crowded expressway, signalling madly and yelling at my kids in the back seat, "Don't talk to me now! I'm driving!" Once, when I was attempting to parallel park next to a coffee shop, I saw a whole group of kopi uncles eyeing me with interest. I'm pretty sure they were taking bets as to whether I would hit the railing, in between sips of their kopi.

I had suggested to Papa that we wrap a giant sponge around the car. After all, Singaporeans are just frightful drivers and as pedestrians, they're not much better. When I'm driving, I'm constantly muttering to myself like an escaped lunatic:

"What, is your signal for decoration?"

"Are you colour blind? Can't see the red light?"

"Mad, park here like it's your grandfather's road."

"Zebra crossing 50m away and you cross here. Feeling suicidal today?"

I've come to the conclusion that driving is like exercising, that is:

1. You get better with practice but may never actually come to enjoy it.

2. Some people just have two left feet—disastrous for both activities.

3. Doesn't matter that you're perfectly coordinated, some idiot can always come crashing into you.

So as I drive my prince and princess around, I chalk it up to another sacrifice I'm making for them. Years from now, they'd better return the favour and preferably not drive me to a nursing home.

Irregular English

Last week as I was walking home with Noah, I attempted to teach him the basic grammar rule of subject-verb agreement, since I noticed that he had been getting it wrong in his school worksheets.

"If there's only one thing, you use 'is', but if there are many things, you use 'are'," I explained. "So, 'one boy is going to the party' and 'many boys are going to the party'."

"Okay." Noah pointed to the field we were walking past. "Look, Mummy, many grass are growing in the field."

Me (hurriedly): "No, no, for things you can't count, you use 'is'. So the grass IS growing in the field."

Noah: "Oh. So the grass and flowers is growing in the field."

Me: "Huh? No! Grass and flowers are two things, so they ARE growing in the field."

Noah (baffled): "But I can't count the grass and flowers!"

Me: "I know. But there are two different items—grass and flowers."

Noah (deep in thought): "So grass and flowers ARE growing in the field. But only flowers IS growing in the field."

Me: "Arrgghhh! No, flowers ARE."

Noah (indignantly): "But you said one thing! And I also can't count the flowers!"

Me (wondering if I should have thought this through first): "I know what I said! Flowers just ARE, okay?"

Noah (looking unconvinced): "What about trees?"

Me: "Trees are."

Noah: "Leaves?"

Me: "Leaves are too."

Noah: "How come you can't count grass but you can count leaves?"

Me (feeling a headache coming on): "Aiyah, it's just like that! Some people long ago decided English would be this way."

Noah (pondering): "Maybe they got tired of counting the grass."

Doh.

Today Noah came home and proudly announced, "Mummy, I finished all my English homework in school. I discussed it with my friends so I'm sure it's correct."

I was relieved. "That's good, you can go play then." As he happily skipped off, I decided to check his worksheet:

Irregular Plurals Singular / Plural	Irregular Verbs Present Tense / Past Tense
One tooth – Many *teeth*	Run – *Ran*
One foot – Many *legs*	Sing – *Sang*
One goose – Many *geese*	Bring – *Brang*
One mouse – Many *meece*	Drink – *Drank*
One sheep – Many *sheeps*	Think – *Thank*
One ox – Many *oxes*	Get – *Got*
One man – Many *men*	Catch – *Cot*
One woman – Many *women*	Lie – *Lied*
One child – Many *students*	Cry – *Cried*
One person – Many *humans*	Fly – *Flied*

I don't know whether to be appalled by his standard of English or relieved that he's not the only clueless one in class!

Miss Independent

Thanks to Good Friday, we had a long weekend and I thought I could relax for a change. No such luck! April told me her teacher had given the class an English project to be completed by the following Monday. Don't teachers understand the meaning of a holiday? It's not an opportunity to pile on more work! That made me terribly grouchy until April announced that she would do everything entirely on her own.

"I'm old enough to plan my own work," she told me, with all the confidence in the world.

"Are you sure?" I was doubtful. She had to write a book review and prepare a presentation board to accompany it. It seemed like an awful lot of work.

"Yes, Mummy," she said dismissively.

I took her at her word and left her alone, figuring that it was time for her to learn to be independent. Friday and Saturday came and went, and April didn't seem to have progressed much. When I questioned her, she replied edgily, "I know what I'm doing, Mummy. Trust me."

I should have known better than to trust a procrastinating 10-year-old because on Sunday afternoon, I found April sitting on the floor amid a pile of construction paper and vanguard sheets, with coloured markers strewn all around her, in tears.

"I've got so much to do! I can't finish it!" she cried.

So it was Mummy to the rescue again. I launched into an exasperated lecture on the importance of time management and not biting off more than one could chew. Then, gritting my teeth, I sat down to help her complete her presentation board.

As I was helping April paste her book review of Madeleine L'Engle's *A Wrinkle in Time* on the board, I did a quick scan of her written work and was secretly impressed. It was quite insightful and articulately expressed. Since April doesn't like to show me her composition books, I hardly ever have the chance to read her writing. I must say, she writes very well for her age. Having blown my hopes for a restful Easter Sunday, at least I'm comforted to know that I have one less area of schoolwork to worry about.

Summertime

Noah has been complaining about Summer a lot lately. According to him, she has been picking on him and playing tricks like poking holes in his favourite eraser, hiding his pencils, placing staples on his chair and putting correction tape over the markings on his ruler.

"Her name shouldn't be Summer," he said savagely. "It should be Thunderstorm!"

I was a little upset by the pranks but Noah was reluctant to have me talk to Miss Wee as he didn't want to be known as the boy whose mum had to come to his rescue. But when he started coming home with pen marks on his uniform, this really vexed me as the marks were impossible to remove.

"Who did this?" I demanded.

"Summer," he replied.

Summer again! What's up with this girl? When the pen marks appeared on a third set of uniforms, I blew my top and wrote a note to Miss Wee in Noah's school diary, telling her about the incident and asking her to manage it.

Strangely, Noah dragged his feet when I asked him the next day whether he had shown Miss Wee the note (that should have been my clue right there). He then said she had reprimanded Summer.

Two days later, I received a call from Miss Wee. "So sorry, Mrs Tan," she said. "I didn't reply to your note earlier as I have just seen it. I questioned Summer and she admitted to drawing on Noah's shirt but said that he had drawn on hers first. Noah didn't deny this when I asked him about it. Apparently, they have been playing tricks on each other for a while now."

My heart sank. Not only was my son the perpetrator of pranks, he had lied to me!

When he returned home from school, he received an earful from me.

"HOW DARE YOU LIE TO YOUR MOTHER, YOU

BAD, BAD BOY!"

He wailed, "I hate Summer! She always makes fun of me. She even made up a song about me and got her friends to sing it!"

"What kind of song?"

In between tears and hiccups, Noah said mournfully, "Noah Tan, rambutan, buys a dress from Isetan."

I choked and beat a hasty retreat. Noah thought I just needed to use the bathroom but the truth was, I was struggling to control my laughter. How does one keep a straight face at something like that? I waited till I could compose myself before I went back to him. I told him it wasn't okay to do mean things back to mean people. If Summer bothered him, he should just inform Miss Wee.

In the meantime, he is banned from computer games for two weeks because lying to your mother is a cardinal sin.

Piano Man

I've started Noah on piano lessons.

April has had piano lessons since she was five. She's a bright girl and I knew she would be diligent about practising. She's doing her Grade Four now and coming along quite nicely, according to Mr Low, her piano teacher.

Noah is a different story. He has a deep-rooted aversion to any form of seatwork so piano lessons have never been on his to-do list. Lately however, I noticed that he liked to hover around when April practised. Then last week, I heard someone tinkling the ivories…and it turned out to be Noah!

Curiously, I asked, "Would you like to learn how to play?"

"I think so."

"Are you sure?" I asked doubtfully. "I don't want to have to chase you to practise. If I let you learn, you'll have to practise at least twice a week without me having to nag you."

"Okay, I'll practise."

That was good enough for me so I called Mr Low and scheduled a piano lesson for Noah. I wasn't expecting much but it was clear from the first lesson that Noah and Mr Low really hit it off. Noah looked forward to his lessons and I often heard giggles and happy chatter emitting from the room during lesson time. Before long, Noah was able to play simple tunes and he seemed to enjoy the process.

After a few sessions, Mr Low told me that Noah was a joy to teach: he was bubbly and fun, but most of all, he had an ear for music. Whatever I was expecting to hear, this was not it. I was completely bowled over. My son was a musical talent? Since when?

Mr Low continued, "Mrs Tan, I want to nurture Noah's interest by teaching him Disney songs. Maybe next year, he can consider taking the Grade One exam."

When April heard Mr Low's praises for Noah, she scoffed, "You? I don't believe you'll last six months. By then, you'll stop practising and say you're sick of the piano."

"Don't discourage him!" I chided. I think she was a little jealous. Mr Low was never as effusive with praise for April.

She may be right though. With Noah's short attention span and track record of never sticking to things, he might tire of the piano soon enough. But for now, I just want to revel in the fantasy that I could possibly have the next Lang Lang on my hands.

Now You See It

I received another note from Miss Wee, saying Noah didn't do his Maths homework again. This is becoming a nightmarish routine.

I confronted Noah. "What did I tell you about doing your homework? Why didn't you do it?"

I was expecting the usual excuses but to my surprise, he looked at me indignantly and said, "I did! I really did! Miss Wee didn't believe me."

"Where? Show me."

He showed me his Maths worksheet. Nothing was filled in. It was completely undone.

I was incensed. "What do you mean you did your home-work? There's nothing here! What did I tell you about lying to your mother?"

Noah stamped his foot. "I did do it! I couldn't find my pencil so I used my Ben 10 invisible ink pen. I told Miss Wee she could shine my special torchlight on the worksheet to see the answers."

This time, I couldn't even make it to the bathroom. The mental image of Miss Wee peering at Noah's worksheet using the dim light of a Ben 10 torch just killed me. I sat down and laughed until I cried. Noah, not quite understanding why the situation suddenly took such a turn but relieved that it had changed in his favour, joined in the mirth with his infectious giggle.

Poor Miss Wee.

TERM 3

Time After Time

When Papa recently returned from a work trip in Bangkok, he brought some interesting knick-knacks for the kids. Among all the gifts he presented, Noah was most enamoured with a watch. It was actually just a regular digital watch, nothing fancy. But it had irresistibly shiny and beeping buttons, quite unlike his old gadget-impoverished watch which had long stopped working.

It took me one whole night to adjust the time correctly as the instructions were in Thai. No skill was required, just the random pressing of different combinations of buttons. I finally managed to do it, but I have no idea how!

Noah has been wearing the watch day and night since

he got it. His Chinese tutor recounted to me how he kept looking at his watch during his lesson, as if willing her to praise its beauty and magnificence.

Aware of what he was after but faking ignorance, she told him to stop checking the time or she would make him remove the watch. She had to stifle her laughter when she saw that he was torn between not wanting to take off his watch and being unable to stop admiring it. Finally, she put him out of his misery by praising the watch profusely.

At night when he lay in bed, he would press the light button repeatedly just to see it light up in the dark. He also loved the stopwatch function which led to a significant increase in our trivia knowledge. We knew, for instance, that it took 12 minutes and 43 seconds to drive from our place to Grandma's, that Mika's song "Lollipop" was all of three minutes, that April took seven minutes and 19 seconds to take a shower, and that he took one hour to finish his dinner (although I was sure he deliberately dragged it out just to see how long the stopwatch could run).

Yesterday, Noah came to me and asked, "Mummy, will you be going out today?"

"Why?"

He handed me his watch. "No more battery, can you change it for me?"

One week. That was all his watch could tahan of his manhandling. Actually, I was surprised it even survived that long!

With a Little Help from My Friends

April has been doing reasonably well in her schoolwork but I can't say the same for her social life. Sometimes, I think tween girls are just a bunch of drama queens. It all started a week ago when she came home from school in hysterics, threw herself on her bed and declared that her life was over.

"What happened?" I asked, alarmed and imagining the worst.

"Lisa won't talk to meeeeeee!"

It's hard to roll your eyes without your kids noticing but luckily, April was too distraught to see my unsympathetic gesture. "Okay, what's wrong?"

After some starts and stops, the story unfolded. Lisa, April's best friend, had a mortal enemy in the class, a girl called Siew Ting. Lisa thought Siew Ting was a rude and selfish loudmouth while Siew Ting thought Lisa was a snobbish, spoilt brat. Recently, Siew Ting started becoming pally with April as they were jointly working on a project, and when they eventually went for recess together, Lisa pronounced April a traitor and breaker of the unspoken best friend code. So she gave April the cold shoulder.

"I said I was sorry," wept April, "but Lisa won't forgive me."

"Lisa can't be a very good friend if she's so petty," I offered.

April wouldn't hear of any allusions to her best friend's character. "She is a good friend! You don't understand anything! I'm the one who was wrong."

I knew better than to try and convince her otherwise. It would only have made her more obstinate. "Tell you what, give Lisa a bar of chocolate tomorrow and tell her you're very sorry."

April looked uncertain but at least she calmed down a little. She agreed to try my suggestion and I was hoping the matter would end there.

No such luck. The next day saw a repeat performance of the waterworks.

"Lisa wouldn't accept the peace offering?" I asked.

"She did," sobbed April.

"Then what's the problem now?"

"I ignored Siew Ting so that Lisa wouldn't get mad. Then Siew Ting told all her friends that I'm too proud to talk to her and her friends, that I think I'm better than them. Now none of them will talk to meeeeee!!"

Oh, for crying out loud! I couldn't contain my tetchiness and told her all her friends were behaving like five-year-olds. "This is such a circus. You should be able to talk to whoever you wish. Now stop this nonsense and go do your homework."

For a few days, April walked around with a mournful expression, like her pet cat had just been run over. Then finally, I saw her familiar smile return. "Everything okay in school?" I asked cautiously.

"Yes. Lisa and Siew Ting are now good friends," said April happily. "They said they just didn't know each other well.

You know what, Mummy? I think they both overreacted. So emo for nothing."

You don't say.

Compre-tension

Noah is not doing well in school. I can understand his struggle with Chinese but last term, the subject he faced the most problems in was English. English!

Sometimes, I think God has a strange sense of humour. Here I am, a journalist by profession, with a son who can't write to save his life. It's like David Beckham's son having two left feet. Not that I'm comparing myself to Beckham.

I don't understand it. We speak English at home and April's English is so strong she's regularly getting her compositions read out in class. Noah, however, can't seem to get a handle on it, especially when it comes to English comprehension passages.

To be fair, the standard of English expected of Primary One kids is really high these days. In my time, you went to school to learn how to read. Now you're expected to know how to read before entering Primary One.

Maybe Noah's problem also has to do with maturity because just the other day, when Noah read "nothing escaped his teacher's eyes", he thought things could literally shoot out of her eyeballs, like in an alien movie.

It doesn't help that his attention span is all of two

minutes. I'm starting to realise that his problem with English comprehension isn't so much about understanding the passage. It is about him having to plough through eight pages of questions before coming to the passage, by which time he has grown so bored that his priority is to finish the paper as quickly as possible.

So throwing all caution to the wind, he would proceed to answer questions not by trying to understand the passage but by harnessing his extremely creative powers (honed from many hours of cartoons and computer games).

I was flabbergasted when I saw a practice paper he did in school. The comprehension passage was about a boy called Pippo who saved the day by using his intelligence. The last question was: "What kind of boy do you think Pippo is and why?"

I don't think Noah even read the passage because his answer was: "I think Pippo is a hippo because it rhymes with Pippo."

There I was yelling at him when really, I was trying extremely hard to curb my desire to laugh. Secretly, I would have given him an A* for creativity, but the big red 'X' next to the answer showed that Miss Wee clearly didn't think the same way.

Another passage talked about a girl who bought a teddy bear as a birthday gift for her brother. One of the questions was: "Why did the sister buy a teddy bear?"

Noah's answer: "The shop did not have any Ben 10."

And then there are always those test-your-vocabulary questions, such as: "What word in the passage has the same meaning as 'lively'?" The correct answer for that particular passage was 'energetic' but Noah had no idea what energetic meant. Heck, he couldn't even remember what 'lively' meant. So he wrote: "The word is 'the'."

I hate to say this but maybe my son needs English tuition.

The Scrabble Fiasco

I decided to institute a weekly family game of Scrabble to inject a slightly more intellectual element into our family time (versus eating and watching TV). I was hoping this would help Noah improve his English.

We agreed not to count the points, so that the focus would be on forming words, not on winning. In a family where everyone hates to lose, counting points would be the surest way to kill the game! The objective in our version of the game is to use all our letters. The only penalty is that the person who finishes last has to keep the game set.

When we first started the game, Noah couldn't catch on to the notion of forming words using his letters. He would say something like, "I want to put 'GOAT' but I don't have the 'G' and the 'T'." After a while, there was slight progress as he figured out that he had to form words using letters he had. He would say, "I can put 'MAN' but I don't know where to put it."

Even though he has since grasped the fundamentals of the game, our sessions are still often more frustrating than fun. Last night's was completely off the wall, to say the least.

Some time into the game:

April put 'GENE'.

Noah did a childish Arabian Nights dance.

April: "It's GENE, not GENIE, silly!"

Later in the game:

Noah: "Is 'DALT' a word?"

Me: "No. Put what you know."

Noah: "How about 'YALT'?"

Me: "PUT WHAT YOU KNOW!"

Noah: "Okay, then 'AT'."

Me (exasperated): "Can you please try a longer word?"

Noah (whining): "I want to put 'PRAY' but the 'A' is there, then the word at the bottom will be 'IYHEROIN'."

Me: *facepalm*

Even later in the game:

April put 'KIN' (turning to Noah): "Do you know what KIN is?"

Noah: "I know, like KING KONG!"

Me: !!!!!!!!!!

Finally, towards the end:

Me (to Noah, trying to speed up the game): "Let me give you a hint. You have a 'U' and an 'A'. You can use the 'Q' here to put 'QUA_'?" I peeked and saw that he had a 'Y'.

Noah: "Hmm…'QUAT'? Wait, I don't have a 'T'."

Me: "No such word! What else?"

Noah: "QUACK?"

Me (glaring at Papa who began to laugh helplessly): "Using what you have!!"

Noah: "I don't know! 'QUAY'?" (pronouncing it as 'kueh')

April (losing patience): "QUAY lah! Like 'Collyer Quay' in the National Day song we sing!"

Noah: "Hah?"

Me: "JUST PUT IT DOWN."

After an eternity, the game ended.

Noah: "Alamak! How come I'm last again? Not fair."

Tuition Nation

Noah's English has not improved. He can't even remember basic grammar and his worksheets are peppered with big red 'X's. I'm tired of seeing Miss Wee's comment: "Can try harder!" on every single one of his English worksheets. It is so discouraging.

After much anguish, I decided that it was in Noah's best interest to go for English tuition. Papa didn't approve. "Ling, you're being kiasu," he reproached. "Noah is only in Primary One. Just make him read more books and he'll be alright."

Easy for him to say! He knows Noah hates reading and with my work, when would I find the time to sit down with Noah and force him to read? Better for him to go for tuition and let the professionals help him. So what if I'm being kiasu? This is Singapore! Everyone goes for tuition.

A colleague of mine recommended A* Tuition Centre. She said they had a good track record and many kids from the Gifted Education Programme were enrolled there. This was mystifying to me. Why on earth would these kids need tuition? No wonder we have become a tuition nation, if even the gifted kids think they need extra help. Now, THAT'S kiasu.

I took Noah down to A* Tuition Centre on Saturday to check out the place. There were huge billboards strategically displayed outside the entrance, showing smiling students who had been top PSLE scorers in past years' exams. The centre was packed. So many kids! On the walls were long lists of the names of kids who had scored 250 and above in the PSLE. It did make me feel more assured.

However, I received two shocks. First, the fees. Golly, do parents really fork out such a fortune for tuition? I was mentally calculating the total cost of sending two children for tuition in four subjects here…my head reeled. Now I see why some people say our education system is not a level playing field. Only the well-heeled can afford this sort of help for their children.

Second shock: Noah had to sit for a test. Have I been

living in a cave all these years? Since when do you need to sit for a test to attend tuition? I was confused but I let the teacher lead Noah to a room.

Half an hour later, he emerged with a furrowed brow. "Mummy, what is 'aftermath'?"

"They asked you that?" I said, startled. "It means the result of something that happened."

"Oh," he replied, looking disappointed.

"Why? What did you write?"

"I wrote 'PE'."

I smothered my laugh under the pretence of a cough. Come on, if Noah knew what 'aftermath' meant, why would he need English tuition?

After a while, the teacher reappeared and told me with a straight face that based on the test results, Noah wasn't suitable for tuition at the centre as the lessons would be too advanced for him. She suggested that I try another tuition centre more suited to his standard.

My cheeks burned. I felt like I'd just been doused with a bucket of reality check. Before coming here, I thought the biggest embarrassment was having a journalist's son go for English tuition. I realised I was wrong. The biggest embarrassment was having a journalist's son turned down for English tuition!

How did we get to this state? Now our kids have to be good enough for tuition? How absurd. Of course the tuition centre can churn out top scorers, since they only accept smart kids to begin with. Luckily, Noah seemed oblivious to the whole situation and was more than happy when I told him maybe English tuition wasn't such a good idea.

I'm not having anyone, least of all a tuition centre, tell my son he isn't good enough. I'll just have to try and teach him myself. I know! I'll make him read more books and he should be alright.

Meet the Parents

Today was Noah's Parent-Teacher Conference and I must say I wasn't very keen to speak to Miss Wee. Judging from the number of complaint notes I have received from her over the past nine months (and the number of complaints I've heard about Miss Wee from Noah), to say the two of them have no rapport would be an understatement. He even refused to give her a Teacher's Day present.

Quite a few parents were already gathered in the class-room when I arrived at school. While waiting for my turn to speak to Miss Wee, I collected Noah's practice test scripts to have a look. Even though the Ministry of Education has scrapped exams for Primary One, the school still holds regular tests to assess the children's standards. Maybe they think that by calling it a 'test' instead of an 'exam', parents will be less stressed out. I don't think parents are that easily fooled.

As I was looking through Noah's papers (and relieved that he didn't seem to have done too badly), I was distracted by the mother sitting next to me. She was dressed in a bustier and a bright pink Juicy Couture mini skirt, hardly appropriate wear for a Parent-Teacher Conference, I thought. She also had on a full face of makeup and fascinating fake eyelashes that made it look as if tarantulas were sprouting from her eyelids. She was eliciting many stares from other parents but she didn't seem to notice as she kept making vexed noises and muttering under her breath.

"What's wrong?" I asked.

"My Summer," she exclaimed, gesturing at her daughter's script. "So careless! Threw away so many marks in her Maths paper."

So this was Summer's mother. Secretly pleased that Noah's nemesis had an Achilles heel, I asked, "What did she get for Maths?"

A dramatic sigh. "Only 95/100."

My internal ray of sunshine quickly flickered and faded as I furtively covered Noah's Maths paper which displayed his score of 82/100. Rain on my parade, won't ya.

I felt better when I met Ming Hao's mother, Mei. Now, here was a kindred spirit. She was like a sparrow—small, upbeat and chirpy. I wanted to hug her when she shared with me her challenges of getting Ming Hao to focus on his studies and how his biggest passions in life were soccer and eating. Finally! Someone who understood! We exchanged phone numbers—I was going to need her help to keep tabs on Noah.

My meeting with Miss Wee went as well as I had expected. Meaning: not good at all. This was the feedback I received about Noah:

- He rushes through his work because his goal is to finish it quickly.
- His English vocabulary is weak.
- In English comprehension, he makes up answers not from the passage.
- He's competitive but only in PE.
- He doesn't file his work.
- He was told to bring a set of files in Week Five, he eventually brought them in Week 10.
- He doesn't pay attention.
- He plays in class.
- He won't stop talking to whoever is next to him.
- His handwriting is so bad he confuses himself.
- His pencil is always blunt.

By the time she had finished talking, I could feel my eyes glazing over. No wonder Noah couldn't focus in her class; even I was struggling not to zone out. Although she was talking about Noah, it felt like I was the one in the hot seat. She probably thought I was a horrible mum for not being able to control my child.

In my head, I was yelling, "He's seven! Maybe you should try encouraging him instead of scolding him all the time!" But being a wuss, I meekly promised that I would keep a closer eye on him and privately thanked God that we were three-quarters through the school year. With any luck, Noah would have a more understanding teacher next year.

TERM 4

He's a Keeper

Noah recounted to me most indignantly, "Miss Wee is so unfair. She always lets the girls go for recess first."

"Why is that?"

"She says they are quieter."

"Is that true?"

"Yeeesss…but STILL!!"

Noah is at that age where he thinks all girls are simply irritating. Even though Summer is theoretically his partner, he refuses to hold her hand when they line up. I'm sure the feeling is mutual.

There is only one girl in his class whom he thinks is alright. That's because she is a bit of a tomboy and sometimes plays soccer with the boys. He paid her the biggest compliment there is on Noah Planet: "She's not really a girl. She's a boy in disguise."

Noah has been coming home with a dirty shirt and pants recently, which irks me because the stains are so difficult to wash out. His uniform gets into this state because he has been playing soccer intensively. His appetite for soccer seems to have grown. He used to just play during recess but now, he plays every chance he gets, even the few minutes before school begins and while waiting for the school bus to bring him home.

Many of his soccer kakis are from different classes, except Ming Hao, which confirms my belief that boys tend to make friends and bond over a common activity. Noah probably doesn't know the names of many of these kids but that is not of significance to him. What's more important is their skill level and their availability. Most of the time, the boys don't have a real soccer ball to play with. They just use whatever they can find; even a plastic bottle would suffice.

I was texting Mei one day to check with her on a school worksheet and she mentioned that Noah was supposedly a much sought after goalkeeper in the soccer gang.

"Why is that?" I asked.

"Oh, I think it's because he's not afraid to fling himself into the path of the oncoming ball. Nothing gets past him."

I guess dirty uniforms are a small price to pay for popularity.

A State of Disorder

Recently, when I was regaling my editor with stories of Noah's antics, he asked, "Ling, I don't mean to be rude but do you think Noah might have Attention Deficit Hyperactivity Disorder?" I told him I didn't think so but he probably had these 10 other disorders:

1. <u>Selective Attention Deficit (SAD) Disorder</u>
   The ability to sit unmoving for two hours in front of an X-Men movie, but the inability to focus on Maths for 10 minutes.

2. <u>Memory Aptitude Deficiency (MAD) Malady</u>
   The ability to remember every line of an advertisement jingle heard a year ago, with accompanying gestures, but not what teachers had said earlier that day.

3. <u>Lack Of Sensory Tracking (LOST) Syndrome</u>
   The ability to lose water bottles, lunchboxes, books, files and stationery in school without any idea how it happened.

4. <u>Broken Channel Disorder (BCD)</u>
   The inability to adjust one's volume such that it is constantly tuned to LOUD, particularly when there's a need to ask questions like, "MUMMY, WHY IS THAT MAN SO FAT?"

5. <u>Snot Magnet Syndrome (SMS)</u>
   Afflicts boys five times more than girls. The magical ability to attract dirt, dust and anything resembling snot, coupled with the uncontrollable desire to spread these to different crevices of the body.

THE GOOD, THE BAD AND THE PSLE

6. <u>Sound Origination Syndrome (SOS)</u>
   Afflicts boys 50 times more than girls. The ability to fart, burp and create a musical assortment of noises from various body parts at will.

7. <u>Total and Irrational Regression in Energy Disorder (TIRED)</u>
   The sudden drop in energy level, often triggered by the tutor ringing the doorbell.

8. <u>Blasted Bladder and Bowel (BBB) Malady</u>
   The strange and instant urge to pee or poop the minute one has left a place with a clean and available toilet, despite having been asked 10 times before, "Do you need to go?"

9. <u>Monosyllable Muttering Syndrome (MMS)</u>
   The highly annoying use of monosyllabic answers to questions, like "yah", "no" and "mmm". Sometimes improvement may be observed in the upgrade to two syllables: "okay".

10. <u>Deliberate Under Hearing (DUH) Syndrome</u>
    The ability to hear the opening of a packet of potato chips two rooms away but not their mother standing next to them, yelling at them to do their homework.

If I were a scientist, I would place priority on curing these disorders. I'm pretty sure they've reached epidemic levels.

Just the Way You Are

I really have a very blur son. Once, someone called on the phone and Noah chatted away animatedly for a full 10 minutes. When he finally hung up, I asked, "Who was that?"

He shrugged. "I don't know."

I was incredulous. "Huh? You talked on the phone for so long and you don't know who it was?"

Noah replied indignantly, "He didn't tell me his name!"

In his world, the name of the caller was a minor, unimportant detail. I told him he should always know who he was talking to, so since then, every time he receives a phone call, he would demand, "Who are you?"

Sometimes, I think it must be great going through life as Noah—never worrying about tomorrow, always living for the moment. He doesn't care what other people think of him, not as a strategy for a happy life but I suspect because it doesn't even occur to him to care.

Just this Monday, Noah told me it was Be Yourself Day at school, so he could wear anything he liked. I recalled reading about it in a note but had misplaced it. Nevertheless, I took his word for it and let him wear his favourite Ben 10 T-shirt to school.

When April came home from school, I mentioned it to her. She exclaimed, "It's not today, it's TOMORROW!" OMG, I almost died. (Note to self: never take Noah's word for anything. Always check with the clued-in older sister.) I pictured him sticking out like a sore thumb in his Ben 10

T-shirt amid a sea of school uniforms.

My dread deepened when April recounted how a girl had gotten Racial Harmony Day mixed up with another day. She started crying because she was so mortified to be in her red cheongsam when everyone else was in their school uniforms. If it had happened to April, she would have been scarred for life.

Imagine my concern while waiting for Noah to return home. When he stepped through the door, I casually asked, "Wrong day?" To my immense relief, he smacked his forehead and laughed, "Yah! It's tomorrow! Hahahaha!!"

Noah has a very infectious laugh, so pretty soon, we were all in stitches. Then he added, "Can I wear my other Ben 10 shirt to school tomorrow?"

It's not often I learn something from Noah but this struck me: when you don't take yourself too seriously, you're more likely to enjoy life to the fullest.

Mugger Mother

I always dislike Term Four as that is when the most important exam—the SA2—takes place. This year, I have two kids' worth of exams to worry about, which is no joke. Even though there are technically no exams for Primary One, Noah still has oral and written tests to prepare for. How these are different from exams, I've no idea.

I was counting on April to be more independent in her

revision so that I could focus on Noah. However, this was not to be. In the few Maths assessment papers that I had given to April, she made countless careless mistakes, which irritated me considerably.

Strangely enough, it seemed like the more I yelled, the more mistakes she made. The last straw for me was when she had worked out the right answer for one of the questions but copied the wrong number onto the answer space. How utterly maddening! Instead of being repentant, April was sullen and kept muttering under her breath, no doubt about me. I really don't know why she has become so uncooperative lately.

I raised the possibility of Maths tuition but April immediately launched into a tirade of how packed her schedule already was. I have to admit it's true. With her after-school activities, Chinese tuition and piano lessons, it would be difficult to find an available slot. Engaging another tutor would also be an additional burden on our household expenditure.

No choice. I had to channel my inner Super Mum. Since I had so much to do, I took leave from work to help the kids with their revision. I served up wholesome meals because I wanted them to eat and sleep well, so that they wouldn't fall ill during this crucial period. I was therefore aggravated to find out that Noah ate popcorn chicken during recess in school.

"You ate fried food in school again?"

Noah protested, "Popcorn chicken is not fried! All the

sauce made it soggy."

facepalm

I told Noah's Chinese tutor to supplement his usual weekly session with a few extra lessons, and made Noah work on some English and Maths assessment papers. As usual, Papa's response was: "Ling, Noah is only in Primary One. Don't be so kancheong."

How can I not feel panicky? Noah makes the silliest of mistakes, not because he doesn't know his work but because he doesn't pay attention. In a school English practice paper, he left out one entire page. In another instance, he even forgot to write his name! For Maths, Noah gets tripped up by his handwriting. His '6' looks like a '0', and his '4' and '9' are interchangeable. It's enough to drive me nuts.

On the day of the first paper, I gave each of the kids a bottle of chicken essence before they left for school. Suddenly, it hit me that this was pretty ironic, considering they had blissfully slept through the night and I was the one who was a zombie.

Lost at Sea

Yesterday was the last day of exams. Finally, freedom!

When Noah came home from school, he asked me, "Mummy, is it 'pink in health'?"

"You mean 'pink of health'? Yes. Did it come out in the test paper?"

"Yes. I wasn't sure if it was pink or orange." Orange!

"Which did you choose?"

"Pink. I guessed lah." He looked at me accusingly. "You taught me blue, red, green, yellow, you never taught me orange!"

As a treat, I took leave today to take the kids to the pool. While we were there, we saw some other children undergoing their swimming survival test.

"Why are they wearing pyjamas, Mummy?" asked April.

"You watch. Later, they will use their pyjama pants as a float. It's so you can save yourself if you're ever lost at sea."

April and Noah observed as one by one, the kids expertly removed their pyjama pants under water, tied the ends of the pants legs together and blew air into them. They then used the inflated pyjama pants as a floating device under their chins.

Noah looked doubtful. "But what if I'm lost at sea and I'm not wearing pyjamas?"

Actually, I sometimes wondered that as well. "Maybe you can do that with other types of pants."

"What if I'm wearing shorts?"

"Weeelll…"

"What about you? What if you're wearing a dress? Or skirt? Or what if you're wearing pyjamas but the dress type?"

"Aiyoh, we won't be lost at sea, okay?! If we ever go on a ship, I'll make sure it's a safe one."

"It's okay. We'll just stay in bed the whole time so we can wear our pyjamas."

Breakaway

Today, the kids received their exam and test results. I was worried for Noah but in the end, he didn't perform too badly. He got Band One for Maths and English (woohoo!) and Band Two for Chinese (expected). He kept crowing that he got full marks for Attendance, until I explained to him that Attendance wasn't actually a subject.

The biggest surprise though, was his English composition. He had been scraping up just 5/10 or 6/10 for his compositions in class so I wasn't expecting the test to be any different. But miracles do happen.

When he saw me, he yelled, "Mummy! Mummy! I got 8/10 for composition!"

I couldn't believe it. Before I could think, I blurted out sceptically, "Are you sure it was '8'? Are you sure it wasn't '6' and you saw the mark wrongly?" Immediately after I said that, I thought, oops, that's pretty insulting.

Thankfully, Noah was oblivious to any slur on his ability and happily replied, "No lah! I thought I would get only 5/10. I didn't dare to look at my paper. Then I peeked and saw, I really got 8/10!" I didn't know how he pulled that rabbit out of the hat but that was jolly good news! I gave him a big hug and told him he was a clever little boy.

April scored more than 80 marks in every subject. However, her Maths result, 83/100, was a drop from last year. "Must be your careless mistakes," I commented. I was astonished when she said resentfully, "How come you praise

Noah when he only did well in compo but you pick on my one not-so-good subject?"

"I'm not picking! I'm just saying. This is Noah's first test. You can't compare this way."

She retorted, "When I was in Primary One, I scored more than 90 marks for every subject. You never praised me like that. It's not fair."

I was stung. "I'm tired of hearing you say things are not fair. I was only asking. You're being too sensitive."

That kind of spoilt the mood for the rest of the evening even though Papa did make a big fuss of both April and Noah when he came home from work.

Much as I hate to admit it, I know April's right. I do expect more from her but isn't that normal? She's so bright and hardworking, it's only natural that I have higher expectations of her. Papa says I sometimes put too much pressure on her. He's one to talk—he leaves all the responsibility of the kids to me! He doesn't even look away from his National Geographic channel when the kids ask him questions, except to say, "Go ask your mother." How many times can one watch salmon swim upstream to spawn? I never realised April felt bad about it though. Maybe I should tone it down a little.

Food for Thought

We usually go out for dinner on weekends and agreeing on a location is often a complicated affair. If it were up to me, I would just make everyone go to a nice restaurant, order for them and tell them to eat up.

However, Papa believes in taking the democratic route and insists on getting consensus from Miss Tree Hugger and Master Junk Food. April is not a fussy eater but ever since she watched a documentary on how meat production contributes to greenhouse gases, she has declared that she would no longer eat red meat.

Which is admirable and everything, except that one of my favourite restaurants is a steakhouse. It's also rather annoying when you're trying to enjoy a lovely, juicy T-bone steak and someone next to you is prattling on and on about how you're a culprit in global warming. I need to bring ear plugs to some of these dinners.

Noah has no such qualms. He embraces meat whole-heartedly, even more so if it's deep-fried and served with a side of French fries. His main quarrel is with vegetables, which he believes are designed only for animals.

He reasons, "If cows eat grass and I eat the cow, doesn't that mean I'm eating my vegetables?"

Or, "Potato is a vegetable, right?" Chomps on a French fry. "See, I'm eating my vegetables!"

Nice try.

Today, after a long, drawn-out argument over where to eat, we ended up at a fish and chips restaurant. No red meat for April, fried food for Noah. As I was observing the two of them eating their fish and chips, it struck me that their gastronomic methods were so indicative of their personalities.

April, the planner, ate all her salad first and left her favourite parts (the fish and the chips) for last. Noah, the instant gratifier, gobbled up the chips like Pacman devouring fruit. He moved on to the fish and finally dawdled over the salad. He then tried to convince me that he was too full to eat it.

"Would you like ice cream after this?" I asked sweetly.

"Yes!" he said, falling for the trick.

"Then you're not too full. EAT THE SALAD."

Noah's love affair with food extends even to his playtime. He plays Restaurant King on the computer and sometimes pretends he's serving up dishes at his own restaurant. Once, he played a waiter and he greeted me, the supposed customer.

"What do you want, woman?"

"That's not how waiters greet their customers!" I protested. "You need to be more polite. Try again."

"Okay. What do you want, lady?"

Anyway, opening a restaurant in the future is probably not within Noah's range of ambitions. As he revealed with candour, "I don't like to cook. I only like to eat."

One need only look at his widening girth to know it's true.

'Tis the Season

The end of the year is always such a great time. No homework to finish, no exams to worry about.

As we were walking along Orchard Road, I pointed to a picture of the silhouettes of Mary on the donkey and Joseph beside her, making their journey to Bethlehem. "Look," I asked Noah, "what does the picture show?"

He replied, "A horse and two men."

I think the spirit of Christmas is somehow lost on him. When he was five, he told his Grandma that the Three Little Pigs brought gold, mud and Frankenstein to baby Jesus. Grandma, an ex-Sunday School teacher, was not amused.

Unfortunately, despite our attempts to educate Noah about Christmas, the season for him mainly revolves around his material desires. This year, he made no secret about his deep admiration for the latest Ben 10 action figure—a giant glow-in-the-dark Diamondhead with a shooting mechanism. Each time we passed by the toy section in a department store, he would look longingly at the display and then proceed to tell me how cool it was, in case I wasn't aware of its splendour.

Eventually I caved and bought it for Noah. It was worth the bomb I spent just to see his face light up like a beacon when he tore open his present on Christmas Day. As he fiddled with the toy, I asked him, "What does it do?"

He looked up and solemnly replied, "It makes me happy."

What a great outlook.

YEAR

2

TERM 1

From This Moment on

Life is a continuum but there's something about the New Year that delineates a new chapter in this ongoing journey.

Maybe it's because my kids are starting yet another brand new school year. April is entering Primary Five. I still remember when she started Primary One. How quickly she has grown! Thankfully, she performed well enough to get into the top class again. As for Noah, this time last year, I was worrying over whether he could cope with primary school. Now, he's starting Primary Two. I know it's a cliché but time really flies.

I love the start of a school year. As I was helping April and Noah get ready—new school bag, new stationery, new books—I realised this ritual of renewal symbolises hope and optimism. It's a chance to wipe the slate clean of old mistakes and make new discoveries. Who will their new teacher be? Which new friends will they make? The anticipation that something good will happen has not yet been squelched by the daily grind.

I made these New Year resolutions:

- Make sure Noah does his homework so I won't get any more notes from the teacher (please let him have a nice teacher this year).
- Make sure Noah practises the piano at least twice a week.
- Make Noah spend less time playing computer games.
- Stop telling Noah his pet frog is slimy and disgusting.
- Give the kids less fast food.
- Make sure the kids take their vitamins.
- Stop nagging April to shower.
- Stop nagging April to tidy her desk.
- Stop nagging April to sleep early.
- Basically stop nagging.
- Yell less.

Okay, some of these are a little ambitious and I'm pretty sure I'll break quite a few of them even before 1 January is over. But I truly want to try to be a better parent. It's a new year—anything is still possible.

Déjà Vu

On the first day of Primary Two, Noah came home and told me very unhappily, "I don't like my form teacher Mrs Goh."

"It's the first day!" I admonished. "You barely know her. You have to give her a chance. Anyway, she can't be as bad as Miss Wee, right?"

Noah looked even more cross and replied, "Mrs Goh IS Miss Wee. She got married in December."

Oops. Darn it.

After dinner, Noah was flipping through his Young Scientist magazine when he came across the word 'dozen'. He asked me what it meant and I wasn't terribly pleased as I remembered having explained it to him not too long ago. His memory is simply atrocious.

"Think about it, Noah," I urged. "Where would you have heard the word 'dozen'?"

Noah furrowed his brow and suddenly brightened up. "I know, like a dozen muffins."

Me: "That's right, so how many is a dozen?"

Noah: "A lot."

Me: "It's a specific number. How many?"

Noah (without hesitation): "Eight."

Me: "No, more."

Noah: "Ten thousand."

Me: *facepalm*

April (chiming in): "It's 12. And do you know what a baker's dozen is?"

Noah (confidently): "Twelve bakers!"

I think it's going to be a difficult year.

Dressed for Success

Chinese New Year came early this year. We barely had time to take down the Christmas tree before it was time to put up the pussy willows. It was a mad rush to get everything ready.

Papa is a firm believer in tradition, especially making sure everyone has new clothes. Then again, he's not the one who has to drag two reluctant kids to mall after mall, trying to clothe them while not getting ripped off by retailers looking to cash in on the festive season.

Am I the only mother in Singapore who hates buying clothes for her children? I wish I could be like Mei. She told me that she simply goes to any local clothing chain when they're having a buy-two-get-one-free promo, buys three sets of identical shirts and pants for her three sons in their respective sizes, and makes them wear the purchases, no opinions entertained.

I don't know how she does it. Maybe her kids are unusually compliant because mine would never stand for it. I've given up trying to buy apparel for April. She refuses to wear what I buy for her and the items sit untouched in her wardrobe until she's outgrown them. Then they're carted off to the Salvation Army, with the tags still attached. Such a waste of money.

The trouble is that lately, she has begun to wear shapeless, androgynous attire almost exclusively. She is always in a dark T-shirt or hoodie and jeans. I miss those days when I could dress her up in pretty frocks and show her off. Now she is repulsed by all dresses, like they are evil incarnate. A few weeks ago, I bought her a lovely floral skirt on impulse. She cringed as if I had gotten her some vulgar Halloween costume.

"Mummy, I'm not wearing flowers on my butt!" she winced.

Sigh. What happened to my little girl who would prance around in a charming pink dress with matching hairclips? She must be having growing pains. All these teen girls— always wearing a multitude of muted shades like they're about to attend a perpetual string of funerals.

Noah is the complete opposite. He wants to stand out and be noticed so he scorns anything dull or drab. His wardrobe reminds me of a box of vibrant poster colours—fire engine red, neon green and radioactive orange. You almost have to wear sunglasses to withstand the visual assault. It isn't too difficult to dress him, except that recently, he insists on wearing only Ben 10 shirts. Do you know how much those cost? Twenty-five dollars for a cotton T-shirt! Highway robbery.

I really should make Noah stop watching those cartoons. It's not the TV time that I object to, it's the associated merchandising that sucks kids and parents into their deep, dark world. After he became hooked on Ben 10, he wanted the Ben 10 water bottle, Ben 10 T-shirts, Ben 10 shoes, Ben 10 action figures and of course, the Omnitrix. For $49.95, it should at least tell time.

Anyway, after spending three hours traipsing the length of Orchard Road, I managed to find something to satisfy everyone. A navy blue blouse for April (she conceded on the pink trim along the sleeves, only because it was for Chinese New Year) and a new pair of jeans. An electric blue Ben 10 shirt for Noah and matching cargo pants. Job done for the year!

Blessed

For our reunion dinner, we usually eat at a restaurant to save Grandma the hassle of cooking. This year, we made reservations at our favourite Chinese restaurant—Ming Jade. In my opinion, it has the best roast duck in Singapore. Just thinking about it makes my mouth water.

A few days before the dinner, April dropped a bombshell. "I'm not eating shark's fin," she proclaimed adamantly. "You shouldn't too. It's so cruel to the sharks."

"It's just once a year!" I tried reasoning with her. "Grandma loves her shark's fin. She'll be so upset!"

"Do you know that they cut off the fins and release the sharks back into the water to die?" she shrieked dramatically.

No amount of cajoling would move her. When April

decides to put on her suit of stubborn armour, she's immovable. How on earth did I raise a daughter like that? The truth is, it wasn't just for Grandma's sake. I love shark's fin soup myself.

Papa said it was good that April was so environmentally conscious and we should stand by her convictions, so he called the restaurant and asked them to substitute the shark's fin soup with fish maw soup. Sigh.

We didn't tell Grandma though, so when the soup was served, I was rather nervous, wondering if she would notice.

"Grandma," April piped up, "how do you like the…"

"SHARK'S FIN SOUP!" I blurted out, shooting a warning glare at April. "It's good, isn't it? Yum."

I hastily drank my soup, averting Grandma's gaze. To my surprise, it really was good. I wouldn't have known it wasn't shark's fin soup if nobody had told me. Maybe I wasn't missing anything after all.

The joke was on me though because when we returned home, Papa disclosed that Grandma had pulled him aside and whispered to him that the restaurant was trying to cheat us because it wasn't shark's fin soup. She didn't say anything out loud because I was clearly enjoying the soup so much she didn't want to break the truth to me.

Sharp grande dame.

On the first day of Chinese New Year, we visited my elderly aunt, whom I hadn't seen for many years as she had just returned from China. Noah had to use the bathroom and when he had finished, he sidled up to me, his eyes wide as dinner plates, and whispered urgently, "There's something in the cup on the sink!"

"What?" I dismissed impatiently.

"It's TEETH!"

I hastily explained that this was not a ghoul house that kept body parts. I wasn't sure if he was more relieved or disappointed that his gentle 80-year-old grand-aunt wasn't really the wicked witch from *Hansel and Gretel* in disguise. Maybe he thought she was urging him to eat all those Chinese New Year cookies to fatten him up for her supper.

My aunt smiled fondly at April and Noah and pushed another tray of pineapple tarts towards them. She then turned to me and said, "Ah Ling, this is the best time. You may not think it now but when they're all grown up, you'll realise it."

I looked at my kids—my headstrong daughter and my guileless son—and I knew she was right. It is a blessed time for me.

I've Got the Music in Me

April predicted it and it has come true. Getting Noah to practise the piano has become a real hassle and I'm tired of having to nag him.

"Noah," I pleaded in despair. "Please, PLEEEAASE can you practise the piano? You promised me you would and now I have to remind you every day!"

"I never wanted to learn!" he pouted. "Why did you make me learn the piano?"

"You asked to!" I retorted crossly. "Don't you remember?"

"You shouldn't have listened to me! I was young and didn't know anything."

If not for the fact that Noah has real talent, I would just let him stop lessons. Mr Low raves about how Noah has a musical gift that should be nurtured. He cleverly picks songs that appeal to kids, like Disney show tunes, and says Noah learns them very quickly. I must admit, I was rather astonished to hear Noah confidently perform the rather complicated theme song from *The Pink Panther* just after six months of lessons.

Mr Low was so taken by his new prodigy that he persuaded me to sign Noah up for the Grade One practical exam later this year. I was swept up by his enthusiasm but now I wonder if I might have been too carried away as Noah is vehemently opposed to practising. The problem is that he plays largely by ear, that is, he memorises where the notes are and what they sound like. Practising for a piano exam means having to actually read the notes, which spells too much work for him.

"Come on, Noah," I appealed. "Don't you think it's great to be able to play music?"

"Yes," he conceded. "But I don't need to learn the piano to do that."

"Why?"

"I can play music on the iPod. No need to practise."

God Bless This Mess

Barely two months after the new school year started, I received a call from Noah's Chinese teacher. Noah had inexplicably ignored the lined squares in his exercise book and his Chinese characters floated, like butterflies, all over the page. The teacher wrote: "I want neat handwriting!" in red ink right across the top of the page. It was even written in English so Noah couldn't feign ignorance.

His English isn't much better. In a recent worksheet on opposites, this was what he came up with:

Fill in the **opposites** of the given words:	
Cold – Hot	Below – On top
Good – Summer	Wake – Sleep
Cheap – Not cheap	Open – Close
Fast – Slow	Buy – Hello
Pretty – Summer	Boy – Girl
Early – Late	Brother – Sister
Day – Nite	Son – Moon
Front – Backside	Friend – Summer

Clearly, Noah's relationship with Enemy Number One has not improved. Looking at his answers, it's just a matter of time before I get a call from Miss Wee…I mean, Mrs Goh.

I had no choice but to make another trip down to the

nearby bookstore to buy more assessment books for Noah. There were throngs of people at the store, mostly parents with sullen children. I could hear many mums reprimanding their protesting kids, "Your comprehension is so bad! This book will help you. And this one. And maybe that one too."

I recently wrote an article for *Realities* on how bookstores around the world were struggling to stay afloat because people were reading less and less. But this local chain is bucking the trend because it sells fiction and non-fiction books as an afterthought. It is really all about assessment books and stationery, and that's a clever business plan if I ever saw one. I have never seen parents so happy to part with their money as they cart off piles of assessment books with accompanying pens and correction tape, in the hope that their blur kids will become geniuses overnight.

But who am I to talk? I'm a regular fixture there and my store discount card has seen more wear than a school teacher's red pen. While I was there, I figured I might as well stock up on April's assessment books. I saw a new series of challenging Maths assessment books based on the latest Ministry of Education syllabus and it looked quite good. Hopefully, April can eliminate her careless mistakes with more practice.

Mother Nature's Son

Today Noah's class went on a school excursion to the Botanic Gardens and I had taken time off work to follow the group as a parent volunteer. I was hoping that my helpfulness would score some brownie points with Mrs Goh so that she could overlook some of Noah's shortcomings.

The bus ride to the Botanic Gardens was mostly uneventful, except for one boy who threw up all over his seatmate's shoes. I saw him wolfing down a whole cream bun just before the journey so I can't say I was surprised.

At the Botanic Gardens, the problems started almost from the get go. After we had alighted from the bus and gotten everyone to line up in pairs, it began to drizzle.

"Boys and girls, put on your raincoats!" instructed Mrs Goh.

A whole lot of fuss ensued with some kids throwing out everything in their bags to look for their elusive raincoats. "I can't find it!" and "I can't button my raincoat!" were common refrains. It took Mrs Goh and me a good 15 minutes to help everyone don their kits, by which time the rain had stopped, to my utter annoyance.

Mrs Goh remained unflustered. "Boys and girls, put away your raincoats!"

Putting away the gear was even worse than putting it on as the kids found it impossible to fold the damp raincoats back into their original compact packages. Most of the children simply stuffed the soggy, crumpled masses into their bags.

When we had finally gotten the class back in order, Mrs Goh led the procession around the gardens, explaining the names of some of the trees and flora. I didn't hear a word because I was bringing up the rear, trying to get the noisy kids to stay together. Suddenly I noticed that Noah, half-way up the line, was alone. His partner was gone.

"Noah, where's Summer?" I asked.

"I dunno," he shrugged. "She saw a squirrel, I think."

"You're supposed to stay with your partner!" I yelled, looking around frantically.

"I don't care! I'm not holding her hand."

Hurriedly explaining the situation to Mrs Goh, I went in search of Summer. Thankfully, I found her not too far away by a gnarly saga tree. *Adenanthera pavonina*, according to the plaque. Not that it mattered to Summer, who was still searching for the mysterious squirrel and looked defiant when I told her she shouldn't have wandered off.

"Now I can't find the squirrel," she said petulantly. Why is it kids these days aren't afraid of grown-ups? Summer has that bossy, know-it-all air about her. She is exactly the kind of person that would push Noah's buttons.

Just as I'd firmly led her back to the group, Summer suddenly yelped, "There's a bee climbing up my sleeve!" Before anyone else could react, Noah sprang into action. "I'll kill it for you!" he pronounced and gave her upper arm a resounding THWACK.

"OOWWWWW!! I'm stung!!" Summer cried out. "You stupid boy!"

An uproar resulted, with all the kids clamouring to see

what was going on and Summer shrieking hysterically. I lifted her sleeve and to my dismay, saw that she had indeed been stung. Her arm was already beginning to swell an angry red. Mrs Goh frowned and said authoritatively, "Mrs Tan, I'll handle this." She then took Summer by the hand and led her to the information counter to get some medical aid.

Meanwhile, I stayed with the kids to maintain order, or what was left of it. The children had grown tired of hanging around and ran off to the nearby open field to play catching. Noah and his buddies found an empty can, and used that as a soccer ball to have a match. By then, I had given up trying to manage the kids so I told myself it was probably best to let them expend their pent-up energy. The weather had also turned scorching hot but I knew my calls for Noah to put on sunscreen would fall on deaf ears.

Summer returned a while later and had recovered from her initial frenzy. She was now ready to translate everything that had happened into the adventure of the day and regaled her friends with a blow-by-blow account of how she had braved the pain when the sting was pulled out with a pair of tweezers. She also made sure to emphasise repeatedly that her predicament was due to "that stupid Noah", to which her friends, rallying together in sisterhood against the idiocy of boys, nodded sympathetically.

Right then, Ming Hao came up sniffling and clutching his hand, explaining that he had sprained his wrist during the soccer match. Back to the information counter Mrs Goh went, this time with Ming Hao. When Noah sauntered up to me and asked whether there was a McDonald's nearby, I lost it and snapped, "No more fast food for you! For the rest of your life!"

After what seemed like an eternity, Mrs Goh reappeared with Ming Hao, his wrist in a bandage. She was still calm but her lips were pursed and she didn't seem very receptive to my apologetic nods. I bet she was thinking that she should screen the parent volunteers for future excursions. Finally she announced to the students in the field that it was time to go and we boarded the bus.

The kids seemed pretty psyched about how a supposedly sedate nature trip had turned out to be so exciting. Summer's adventure was all they could talk about on the bus. As for me, I was nursing a headache and mentally crossing off "parent volunteer" on my to-do list.

That evening, I discovered that I was horrendously sunburnt on my nose and scalp, while Noah was perfectly fine. No brownie points for me.

Earth Song

Last Saturday, the world celebrated Earth Hour and April, the greenie, insisted that we did too. Earth Hour is an annual international event that calls for households and businesses around the world to turn off non-essential lights and electrical appliances from 8.30pm to 9.30pm, to raise awareness for the need to act in order to stop climate change.

Unfortunately, in our household, only April and Papa have any sort of environmental awareness and conscience. Mine is borne more out of my desire to be supportive of April's causes and Noah…well, Noah is Noah.

April: "We have to turn off all our lights for one hour."

Noah: "Okay, I can still play Restaurant King in the dark."

Me: "And I can watch TV."

Papa: "Ling, we're supposed to turn off all electricity! That means no computer and no TV."

Me (alarmed): "What? I thought it's just lights?"

Noah (equally alarmed): "Hah? Can't turn on the air-con too?"

April (exasperated): "We're supposed to save the earth!"

Me: "Then what are we going to do, just sit around in the dark for one hour?"

Noah (persistently): "Without air-con?"

In the end, we sat in the living room in the dark with one lit candle from 8.30pm to 9.30pm. We played word games and had April attempt to explain global warming to Noah. As she got to the subject of climate change and how carbon dioxide heated up the earth, Noah grew increasingly confused. When she eventually explained that rearing cows for food added to the earth's pollution because of the methane from cows' farts, Noah nearly fell backwards in astonishment.

"So now you know why some people refuse to eat meat?" asked Papa.

"Yes!" replied Noah, his eyes wide with disbelief. "Because the cows are smelly!"

TERM 2

Physical

Last week, after his school health check, Noah brought home a form to say that he had to join the school's Fitness Club. I was not fooled—I knew that was just a nice way of saying that he was overweight. It was a wake-up call for me. I always knew he was a little chubby but I figured that since he was so active, he would automatically shed the weight. Now I'm thinking maybe he does have a problem.

The trouble is, Noah is too fond of his food and when I'm too tired to cook or have to stay late at the office, I would often grab some fast food on the way home. I really should stop doing that. It's convenient but oh, so diabolical in terms of nutrition. Even when we go out on weekends to hawker centres, Noah gravitates towards all the unwhole-some foods—chicken rice, char kway teow, grilled chicken wings and his absolute favourite, roti prata.

Once, he told me he wanted to be a doctor when he grew up.

"Why?" I asked, delighted and thinking my son finally had big ambitions and noble dreams.

"Doctors have the best job. They have to eat a lot of ice cream to get all those ice cream sticks."

No wonder Noah had seemed so enthralled when the doctor used the tongue depressor to check his throat.

I know as parents, we should set a good example when it comes to diet but it's so difficult. Why does unhealthy food always taste best? I never crave yong tau foo the same way I hanker after satay beehoon. Sigh. Thank goodness April has managed to cultivate healthy eating habits, in spite of us.

Putting aside my pride, I had to admit that joining the Fitness Club would probably be good for Noah. The Fitness Club was also a CCA and joining it would expose Noah to different sports, including floorball, table tennis, badminton and soccer. It took place twice a week after school and would certainly help him get into better shape. He would need to join a CCA by Primary Three anyway, so this was probably a good one to consider.

After the first session yesterday, Noah told me Fitness Club was fun. He played floorball for the first time and enjoyed it tremendously, especially since Ming Hao had also been roped into the club. Fat birds of a feather flock together.

He told me with glee, "I'm not so good yet since I've never played floorball before, but when we play soccer, we will trash everyone!" Yes, my little Messi with the big ego. As long as it helps him lose that spare tyre, I'm not complaining.

One Marshmallow, Two

I was searching the Internet for ways to improve my kids' academic performance when I came across an article on the Marshmallow Experiment, conducted in the 1960s at Stanford University. Some four-year-olds were given a marshmallow and promised a second one if they waited 20 minutes before eating the first one. As expected, some children were able to wait and others could not.

The researchers followed the progress of each child into adolescence and discovered that those who waited were assessed to be better adjusted and more dependable, according to their parents and teachers. Even more revealing was the fact that these kids eventually scored significantly higher on the SATs in high school, giving them an advantage in admissions to Ivy League universities. Basically, individuals who were willing to put in the effort before seeing rewards were more sensible and performed better in school.

What surprised me was that this personality trait could be identified as early as four years old. That made me very worried as I knew Noah was always living for the moment and unable to wait for his rewards. April, on the other hand, was fine, since she was the Queen of Delayed Gratification. She practically lives by the old Chinese adage—先苦后甜—tasting the bitter before the sweet.

To test Noah, I asked him what he would do in the marshmallow situation.

Me: "So would you eat the marshmallow or wait to have two?"

Noah: "None."

Me: "Huh? Why?"

Noah: "I don't like marshmallows."

Me (impatiently): "Okay, let's say it's something you like to eat."

Noah: "I still won't eat it."

Me (mystified): "Why?"

Noah: "I don't know the man! Maybe it has poison."

Me: "Gnnnnggghhhh! Okay, imagine it's not something to eat but something you really like. Say a very special Ben 10 action figure."

Noah (perking up): "Is it Ultimate Big Chill?"

Me: "Whatever! So will you take it first?"

Noah: "I'll wait until the man gives up."

Me: "You're not answering my question! Will you take it or wait for another one?"

Noah: I'll snatch both and run away."

Luckily, the researchers never had Noah participate in the experiment. He would have completely skewed the results.

Sharpest Pencil in the Box

Mr Low has started teaching Noah music theory and he's really particular about having sharp pencils. I guess you can't blame him. When you see the shapeless, audacious blobs that Noah lackadaisically draws on his manuscript book, it's hard to decipher whether the note is on the line or in the space. Usually, it's somewhere in between, not quite acceptable when you're dealing with something as precise as musical notation.

"Mrs Tan, can you make sure Noah has a sharpened pencil ready for his lessons?" Mr Low requested. It sounded easy enough but I swear, the pencils unsharpened themselves. By the time Mr Low's weekly visit came around again, the only available pencil was the blunt one! And of course the sharpener was missing.

So Mr Low tried another tack: he asked me to get Noah a mechanical pencil. Which I did, except, somehow the mechanical pencil always disappeared. I suspect there's a Stationery Bermuda Triangle in my home. I bought Noah three mechanical pencils on three separate occasions—I even made him pay for one himself as a punishment for losing the other two.

Mr Low is a super nice guy. He never once told me off, even though he must have privately questioned my ability to provide for my children. I mean, he was only asking for a pencil, for crying out loud.

Finally, after many weeks of this rigmarole, he came bearing a gift for Noah—a sharpener. Not just any old sharpener but a GIANT sharpener with moving parts! Noah loved it. Since then, he's been asking for pencils to sharpen all day long.

Now I'm afraid all the pencils at home will be sharpened to stumps in no time!

In My Room

The fights between April and Noah had been intensifying of late, to the point where it was creating a lot of tension at home. Since April turned 11 a few weeks ago, I have noticed that her temper has grown infinitely worse and she has become sensitive to every slightest bit of criticism, even imagined ones. She must be going through puberty. I hope she outgrows this phase soon because she has become very difficult to be around.

I discussed this with Papa and he felt that it was time for the kids to have their own rooms. I agreed. The close proximity between April and Noah exacerbated the situation and since Noah was your typical clueless boy with no regard for personal space, he often ended up bearing the brunt of her rage.

I can't say I blame April for losing her cool sometimes. Noah would do inexplicable things like use her books as mountain terrain and her soft toys as prisoners of war for his make-believe battle scenarios. When April discovered 'blood' stains on her favourite stuffed rabbit, World War Three erupted and I had to physically separate the two kids before they came to blows. I also learnt, too late, that it was unwise to let a seven-year-old boy have access to permanent markers.

In addition, Noah has an unfathomable compulsion to irritate April just to provoke a reaction. Once, after his shower, he streaked stark naked out of the bathroom and into their room, and proceeded to perform a silly dance in his birthday suit. This triggered a shriek from April, "AARRRGGHHHH!!! My eyes! I need to bleach my eyes!"

The third bedroom in our five-room HDB public housing flat had been used as a study and my workplace away from the office, but it was time for me to give it up. We decided to move my work stuff out of there and Noah's bed in. I would just have to write in the living room.

After we told the kids they would be getting their own rooms, they became super excited about it. April started marking down the days on her desk calendar, with a big circle and happy face around the move date. Noah was so stoked he started calling me at work several times a day to say, "I can't wait till I have my own room!" I grew so sick of hearing about it that I eventually barked, "If you don't stop saying that, I'm going to take it back!"

Moving day was exciting, with both kids not squabbling for once. April even helpfully offered to transfer all of Noah's toys to his room for him. I think she couldn't wait till every trace of him was gone from her room.

The instant Noah's room was set up, he pasted a sign on the door: "Noah's Room. If you want to come in, knock on the door!" He took this notice very seriously. On the first day, I walked into the room unannounced and he looked rather piqued.

"Mummy, you didn't knock."

"The door was open! Anyway, you don't knock when you come into MY room."

"That's because you didn't put up a sign!"

The rule is: you have to knock if you wish to enter his room. You then have to wait for him to ask, "Who is it?" and you have to respond before he would permit you to go in. This rule applies even if the door is wide open and he can actually see you standing in the doorway. Heck, it doesn't even matter whether he is in the room or not. Once, he was in the living room and saw April march straight into his room. He yelled across the hall, "YOU DIDN'T KNOCK!"

The room change was an undeniable success though. Tempers have flared less often and April seems happier now that she has a tween-dom to call her own. Noah, too, relishes the fact that he can lay down his hundreds of little toy cars on the floor of his room without having his sister kick them out of alignment and screech at him for setting up a minefield.

It was a picture of peace and harmony until a week after the arrangement. Noah sidled up to me despondently and said, "I'm quite lonely sleeping in my room by myself. Can Jie Jie sleepover with me?"

Doh.

A Mathematical Certainty

I ran into an old friend of mine one day and she asked my kids how old they were. "Seven," replied Noah. "Eleven," said April. Noah then made a monkey face and sang out, "7-eleven. It's a store and more."

My friend was so tickled she couldn't stop laughing. "Life with this one must be a hoot!" she commented.

Yup. It's like living in a comic strip.

If only finding out ages in Noah's Maths problem sums was as straightforward. Just the other day, Noah was trying to do a problem sum which entailed finding out the age of Bobby. I was perplexed as to why he couldn't solve it as he had done similar sums many times before. Finally I led him step by step until he arrived at the answer.

Noah (incredulously): "Bobby is 66 years old?"

Me: "Yes."

Noah: "He can't be 66 years old!"

Me (puzzled): "Why not?"

Noah: "Because Bobby is a boy's name! How can he be an old man?"

Me (amused): "So if a boy called Bobby grows up, what should he be called?"

Noah (thinking for a bit): "Bobbious!"

He had gotten the correct answer but assumed it was wrong because in his understanding, someone named Bobby couldn't possibly be that old.

However, his quirky creativity never fails to entertain me. One of the Maths topics in Primary Two was Shapes and Patterns, and in a school worksheet, there was this question:

> Draw one figure that has 3 straight lines and 4 curves in the box below. Use a ruler to draw your straight lines.

I burst out laughing when I saw what Noah had drawn:

It's such a simple drawing but it characterises Noah through and through. There are times when I worry that he is losing his carefree nature to this pressure-cooker academic rat race, and I wish there could be a kinder system that would allow him to grow up at his own pace. But little things like this assure me that his spirit isn't so easily quashed.

I'm glad Noah can find his own way to express his personality even within something as structured as the Singapore school curriculum.

Us Against the World

April's SA1 is in two weeks and it has been a very gruelling time for both of us. Since she is already in Primary Five, the crucial year before the PSLE, I feel that she should be improving on her answering techniques. Unfortunately, she is only doing well in English. She doesn't seem to be making much progress in the other subjects, especially Maths. She knows her work reasonably well but she is so prone to careless mistakes that she tends to lose marks for no reason. I set her only a few sums as practice yesterday, since she had a lot of homework, but she still managed to make several needless errors.

"How can you get your A* in Maths if you're so careless?" I harangued. That, of course, led to one of our classic mother-daughter blow-ups with lots of talking back (April), yelling (me), tears (April), sulking (April) and head-on-wall banging (me). Is it going to be this way right through to the PSLE? I am exhausted just thinking about it.

Papa constantly tells me I'm being kiasu but he's hardly involved in the kids' daily work so he doesn't realise how much needs to be done just to keep up. When Noah doesn't do his homework, I instantly get a note or call from Mrs

Goh. If I don't push April to do more assessment books, her marks drop and she gets disparaging comments on her paper, like "Can do better" or "Try harder". Then she risks being streamed out of the top class.

When the exams draw near, my kids bring home notes from school, asking me to sign an acknowledgement that I would ensure they study for the exams. I suppose it's part of the Ministry of Education's efforts to get parents to be 'partners in education', but it feels more like I'm being arm-twisted into becoming partners in crime. If my child fails, it's somehow my fault.

Our education system doesn't allow kids to grow up at their own pace. Nowadays, the pathways are defined earlier and earlier. If they don't do well in the PSLE, it means they can't get into a top secondary school, and with the introduction of the Integrated Programme, not getting into a top secondary school means their chances of getting into a top junior college and university later on have drastically shrunk. Everything our kids do now has implications later on. That's why it's better to be kiasu now than to regret later.

Colin, a colleague of mine who writes a food column, used to tease me about how kiasu I was when I took leave to help April with her exams. Before his son entered Primary One, he was the biggest critic of kiasu parents. His philosophy was: why succumb to pressure? We have a choice. There are more important things in childhood, like learning how to fish, play soccer and daydream. No need to do assessment books, tuition is overrated, blah blah blah.

The funny thing is, by the time his son was halfway through Primary One, he was completely stressed out by calls from the teacher telling him that his son could not keep up with the work. His son had also become very demoralised because he was placed in a class with the slower learners. Colin then switched to a part-time position, coached his son at home and sent him for Maths tuition! Just last week, he proudly told me that he had discovered a great method of explaining Maths models and that his son had scored 94/100 for his latest Maths test. I wasn't very gracious—I did the whole 'I told you so' routine.

See? It's the system. It turns parents into monsters.

A Day in the Life

Finally, it's the June holidays! But if anyone thinks a mum's life gets easier during the break, they should have their heads thoroughly examined.

8.15am: Crawl out of bed. I really should stop going to bed at 2am.

8.30am: Poke head out of the bedroom door and yell at the kids to get ready.

8.39am: Yell at the kids to put on their shoes because we're out the door in one minute.

8.40am: Leave the house.

8.41am: Turn back to retrieve car keys.

8.55am: Drop Noah at school for Fitness Club. Shout last-minute instructions at him from the car window.

8.56am: Drive April to the chalet. Lucky girl is attending a sleepover party with her girlfriends. Proceed at snail's pace because I've never driven this route before.

9.15am: Reach destination unscathed, hooray!

9.30am: Finally arrive at the chalet on foot, slightly winded. Parked at the wrong place, darn it.

9.40am: Leave the chalet, feeling somewhat sentimental over April's first night away from her family.

9.55am: At the office. Have a big mug of 3-in-1 coffee.

10.10am: Finally can settle down to write.

10.30am: Get call from Noah. Session ended early because only three kids turned up. Darn it!

10.35am: Tell the editor I'm working from home for the rest of the day.

10.40am: Leave to pick Noah up. Mutter at the crazy pedestrians playing Russian Roulette by stepping off the kerb in front of my car.

11.00am: Have a chat with the teacher on Noah's progress. Scribble down all the upcoming changes in the Fitness Club holiday schedule.

11.15am: Buy burgers for lunch en route home.

11.30am: Marvel at an elderly man who proceeds to cross the road despite seeing my approaching car, waving his walking stick at me menacingly the whole time.

11.45am: Arrive home. Send Noah to shower. Remind him he has to practise the piano before lunch.

Noon: Rap on the bathroom door and yell at Noah to hurry up. Taking a luxury spa bath isn't going to get him out of practising the piano.

12.15pm: Sit down at the computer to write.

12.20pm: Get up to yell at Noah for kicking the piano.

12.45pm: Lunch.

1.10pm: Sit at the computer. Really should start work now.

1.11pm: Oh wait, forgot to assign Noah his Maths revision homework.

1.20pm: Go back to the computer. Open several emails from my editor asking when he can expect his article.

1.22pm: Major panic. Attempt to start writing. If only I can get rid of this writer's block.

1.30pm: Mojo flowing now. Come on, keep at it.

2.30pm: Break to mark Noah's Maths assessment paper. Mutter under my breath over silly mistakes.

2.45pm: Go through Maths paper with Noah. Before I start, Noah says, "Mummy, can you not say 'tch' when I get something wrong? I don't like it." Yikes, guilty as charged.

3.00pm: Fall asleep. 3-in-1 has limited potency. Or maybe I shouldn't go through test papers on my bed.

4.05pm: Wake up with a start. That can't be the time????? @*&!@%$!! Scramble to start work. Feverishly. I'll have another mug of that 3-in-1.

5.15pm: Phew! Manage to finish the article. Send it off to editor. Amazing what a looming deadline can inspire.

5.20pm: Drive Noah to get his hair cut. Seriously, I feel like I'm participating in a live video game where you manoeuvre the car to avoid zig-zagging pedestrians. Wasn't there a recent report in the papers about the increase in jaywalkers? I swear half of them live in my neighbourhood.

6.00pm: Hair cut done, ooh…Lionel Messi, look out! Off to have dinner at the nearby hawker centre. Char kway teow with all the crispy lard bits. Never mind—Noah went for Fitness Club this morning. I know I didn't, but doesn't driving count as exercise? Teh tarik to wash it all down—love the frothy bubbles in my favourite local tea!

7.20pm: Home. Put on all my persuasive charm to cajole a pouty Noah to do a couple of English worksheets, reminding him that it's less than five months to the year-end tests.

7.30pm: Get SMS from April: "Just had dinner. Having a great time."

7.50pm: Mark English worksheets. Terribly worried over the mistakes. Go through worksheets with Noah, trying very hard to reign in the 'tch'.

8.30pm: Fetch Papa from MRT station. Very happy it's my last drive of the day.

8.50pm: Chillin' time. Wonder what April is doing.

9.30pm: Send Noah off to bed. Hugs and kisses. "I love you, Mummy." He truly is a sweet kid.

10.00pm: Do the laundry, ironing and plan tomorrow's meals. I hate housework with a vengeance.

11.30pm: Me time! The rest of the household is out like a light (well, except for April who I'm sure won't be getting much sleep tonight). Alternate between watching *The Big Bang Theory*, clearing emails and surfing the web.

1.00am: I'm wide awake. That teh tarik sure has kick!

1.55am: Decide to go to bed. Technically, it's not 2am yet, right? I'm sure I'll be fine tomorrow…I mean today.

TERM 3

Dollars and Sense

Noah has been grumbling that I haven't been giving him enough pocket money. It's not true! I give him enough to buy his food and drinks. April had the same amount at his age and never complained.

"Don't you have enough to eat?" I asked.

"Yes," he replied. "But after I spend my money on food, I don't have any more to buy potato chips for my friends."

Oh, I see. I shouldn't be surprised. Noah has a very generous spirit so I imagine he would love to be able to lavish his friends with snacks. He even lends them comics that he has not yet read. No wonder Ming Hao's mother, Mei, tells me he's very popular in class.

It's not that I'm stingy but I feel strongly that my kids should learn how to manage their money. I shudder when I hear of all those young adults who chalk up debts like there's no tomorrow and expect their parents to bail them out.

I want April and Noah to realise that money is a commodity that needs to be earned and should be used with thought. In this respect, both of them have been well trained. If we enter a toy store, they know better than to badger me to buy something for them. My rule is that I'll pay for necessities. Extras come out of their own pockets except for the occasional treat that I initiate.

Still, even though they were both brought up the same way, their treatment of money differs. April plans for the future, Noah lives in the now. I once took Noah to the bookstore and told him I would buy him only one Tintin comic. If he wanted more, he had to pay for them himself.

Immediately, he said, "Okay! I have $40 in my piggy bank. How many comics can that buy?" I was a little miffed. Somehow the point of valuing money was lost if he was so willing to part with it.

But a friend recently made me think when she told me, "Saving money is not the same as hoarding money." To Noah, money is only a means to an end and even though he values money, he does not love it, which I guess is an admirable trait.

Yesterday, Noah asked me, "Mummy, do you know what I want to be when I grow up?"

"What?"

"A millionaire."

Looks like he has found the solution to his problems.

Roll over Beethoven

Noah sat for his Grade One piano practical exam and that in itself was an achievement of sorts. The preparation leading up to the exam was a mixed bag of frustration and wonder. At first, getting Noah to learn the set pieces was an aggravating process as he simply didn't have the determination or patience to work out the details. He would sit at the piano reluctantly and try out a few notes, not by reading the score but by guesswork. When that failed to work, he would throw a tantrum and kick the piano. I have scolded him countless times for abusing the poor instrument.

However, once he had gotten the hang of it, acquiring the nuances was surprisingly easy. Noah understands how to achieve the required phrasing and tone quite instinctively, which Mr Low attributes to his musicality. It also helps that Noah enjoys performing and I think he is secretly pleased that he has found something he is good at.

"Mr Low says I am a musical pattern!" he boasted to April.

"Talent, not pattern, you idiot!" she derided, rolling her eyes. "And your only talent is being a pest."

Noah even occasionally offers to play for me (he loves an audience, especially an admiring one) and I realise that his personality emanates from his piano playing—sure-footed, fearless and spontaneous.

When Mr Low told me that Noah had achieved Distinction for his piano exam, I was ecstatic. What an accomplishment! I thought it was a great boost to Noah's morale and hopefully, it sent him the message that if he works hard at something, he can do well.

Noah telephoned his grandmother to tell her the good news. "Grandma, Grandma, I got Distinction for my piano exam!" Pause. "That means I passed, you know."

Mr Low was so pleased with Noah's performance, he offered him a reward. "What would you like?"

Noah didn't need to be asked twice. "A lollipop. A big, colourful one." My boy has simple pleasures!

Party Animal

I received another call from Mrs Goh, complaining that Noah didn't hand in his homework and was constantly daydreaming. I'm getting calls from her so frequently, I think she has my number on speed dial.

Only three weeks to the year-end exams! I gave Noah a stern lecture and stressed the importance of focusing in class, especially with his first exam coming up. As always, when he was scolded by me, the corners of his mouth turned down in a very sorrowful manner and his big doe-like eyes filled with tears like he was terribly remorseful, but in truth, I don't know whether he retained anything I said. Five minutes later, he was cheerfully playing with his toys.

I understood why he was more distracted than usual. His birthday party was today and he had been looking forward to it for the longest time. Since I threw a party for April's eighth birthday, it was only fair that Noah got one when he turned eight. What I was about to find out though, was that organising a party for eight-year-old girls was quite different from organising one for eight-year-old boys. It was like comparing a cuddly kitten with The Incredible Hulk. Luckily, I was new to this and didn't know what I was getting myself into.

I was just a teensy bit apprehensive about having 15 wired, hyperactive boys tearing about in our flat. Papa appointed April as referee, authorising her to give the yellow card to any boy up to mischief, like kicking the TV, throwing food or trying to kill Noah's pet frog.

An hour before the party, I received a phone call from a mother of one of the party guests, asking whether I was having balloon sculpting, a bouncy castle or a magician. She sounded disappointed when I said no to all three. Seriously? Parents call to check out party itineraries these days?

When it comes to parties, I'm pretty old school. I love the genuineness of a wholesome party, not the flashy modern ones, so I was going with traditional party games. Only two though because they were recycled from April's party three years ago.

Ming Hao was the first to arrive. "He just couldn't wait and had to come here early!" Mei explained. The party started innocently enough, when a couple of other boys showed up and Noah led them to his room where they kicked a balloon around. Soon, more boys arrived and before you could say "boo", the situation degenerated into mayhem, with boys tumbling over one another, throwing toys at each other while screeching and laughing at the top of their lungs. The mother who had called earlier also brought her younger four-year-old son, uninvited, who proceeded to whirl around the house like a tornado.

April took one look at the pandemonium and retreated to the sanctuary of her room, not emerging until the party was over. Referee, my foot.

Worried that the neighbours might report me to the police for disturbing the peace, I announced that it was time for games. The first game was 'Pin the Tail on the Donkey'. At April's party, it was a snap getting the girls to sit down obediently and take turns in an orderly fashion. No sweat.

In today's case, it took a full 10 minutes just to get the boys to calm down and sit within the game area. Then everyone demanded to go first (I think this is the male 'can't wait' gene). As each boy took his turn, the others crowded around and shouted instructions like "lower!" and "to the left!" to the participant. My persistent "No helping! No helping!" was systematically ignored. Although I must say it didn't really matter because while some boys were shouting 'real' instructions, others, in an attempt to prevent their friends from winning, were trying to mislead the participant by yelling 'fake' instructions. All in all, it was utter confusion.

The second game was called 'Mummy'. The boys were divided into three teams and each team was given a toilet roll. One team member was the mummy and the other team members had to use the toilet roll to 'wrap' their mummy. The team with the best wrapped mummy was the winner.

I don't know how I even got them to understand the instructions. I was hollering at the top of my voice and I still couldn't be heard over the boys' chatter which was louder than 50 hyenas having a family reunion. Mei told me later, "I feel sorry for their teachers!"

The competitive spirit of the boys was hampered only by their lack of planning abilities. Ming Hao's group, in the absence of foresight, chose Ming Hao as the mummy but his generous breadth meant that the team members ran out of toilet paper even before they had covered half of him. Another group's mummy decided midway that he was thirsty and wandered off half-wrapped to get himself a drink, deaf to his team-mates' loud protests. Meanwhile, Noah was shouting haphazard orders at his team-mates who decided it would be easier to fling toilet paper squares at their mummy, hoping they would magically stick. After the game had concluded, the boys immediately launched into a toilet paper fight. I so should have seen that coming.

Then it was time for pizza and cake. The candle-blowing ritual had to undergo a retake because the four-year-old party crasher blew out the candles the first time, even before the birthday song had ended, triggering loud protests from the birthday boy.

Finally, I played a Ben 10 DVD and commanded the boys to gather around the TV, not because they needed a rest but because this mummy did. The party was tough on me but it was a big hit with the boys and Noah enjoyed himself thoroughly.

I'm happy to say that:

1. nobody broke anything; and
2. he's not getting another party next year.

Happy birthday, Noah!

Complicated

It was April's Parent-Teacher Conference today and for the most part, her teachers had great things to say about her. Her English teacher especially, was unreserved in her praise of April's writing abilities. In fact, she wanted April to try out for a couple of national writing competitions. Naturally, I was elated. I hadn't realised how far April had come in terms of her writing.

April's Chinese and Science teachers gave positive feedback too. Even though she was not as strong in these two subjects as she was in English, the teachers felt that her attitude and work ethic would carry her far.

I saved meeting April's Maths teacher, Mr Prakash, for last because I wanted to have a longer chat with him regarding her constant careless mistakes. The conversation didn't exactly proceed the way I thought it would, though.

"April's a very hardworking girl and she does well in class," he assured. "However, she seems to be overly nervous when it comes to exams and her results always end up below her usual standard."

"It's the careless mistakes!" I insisted. "That's why I need to know how I can help her correct them."

Mr Prakash stared at me from behind his tortoiseshell glasses. "It's more than that, Mrs Tan. Do you know that your daughter has a fear of failure?"

What? Fear of failure? What's that got to do with Maths?

Mr Prakash has a slow, deliberate manner and he explained that in a chat he had with April, he realised that her fear of not doing well in Maths had become a stumbling block, so much so that her frame of mind in an exam became unstable and caused her to blank out because she lacked the confidence to do well.

My mind was in a whirl. Was he saying my daughter had a mental problem? What nonsense! Maths teachers shouldn't try to be psychiatrists.

"Isn't being nervous for an exam normal?" I asked

sceptically. "I would have thought the way to solve this is to make sure that she knows her work better so as to build her confidence."

"Well, that's true too…" Mr Prakash replied diplomatically. "I just feel that maybe she can overcome her psychological barrier if we encourage her more and focus less on her mistakes."

'We'? Right. I knew he meant me. He thought I was the one who was not encouraging her and focusing too much on her mistakes. Politely, I thanked him for his time but inside, I was seething. Of course I have to focus on the mistakes! How else would she correct them? What is the point of focusing on all the things she does right? Not wanting to fail just means April aims to do well in life. I don't see what is so bad about that. It's a simple case of a teacher trying to assign blame to the parent instead of taking responsibility for his student's results.

I didn't tell April about the meeting with Mr Prakash because I didn't want to upset her. It doesn't matter anyway. If he won't do anything to help, I'll just have to continue tutoring her myself.

A Ling-uistic Challenge

Since Noah's composition test was coming up, I decided to give him a writing assignment for practice. To my utter frustration, he immediately started whining and crying. At first, I tried being nice and encouraging but after tolerating 20 minutes of complaints and kicking the table, I'd had enough.

Exit nice Mummy, enter fire-breathing Tiger Mum. "If you don't stop whining and get to work, I'm banning you from computer games for the rest of the year!"

I don't know how he managed to write anything amid the torrent of tears. He was howling as if someone had unleashed a sledgehammer on all his favourite toy cars.

This was the four-picture composition question I assigned:

After one hour, this was what Noah came up with:

"Ring! Ring!" the bell of Sunshine primary School rang. Finally it was the school hollidays and Sam could play soccer! He saw his classmates playing soccer in the feild. He asked John can I join? John said no you are a fatty fatty bom bom. You cannot run. you can be our soccer ball. John had hurt Sam's feelings.

Sam sat on the grass at the side. He watched them play the game and John kicked the ball to the midfeilder and pass to the stricker and the stricker kicked very hard and GOAL!!! Suddenly, a furious fox came to eat Sam for lunch. Sam ran to John and shouted "Got fox! got fox! Run!" Everybody ran diffrent places. The fox chase after Sam. John and me ran up the tree. I was very sad so I cried. The fox decided to not have me for lunch so it walked away. John said I am a cry baby.

I stared at the composition for a full 10 minutes, aghast, wondering whether to laugh or cry. Where to even begin? A furious fox that ate children? Cartoons clearly made a deeper impression on Noah than National Geographic. I suddenly remembered that when I was pregnant with Noah, I was reading copious amounts of *Calvin and Hobbes* comics and wishing that my unborn son would be exactly like the rebellious but precocious Calvin. No wonder people say "Be careful what you wish for."

Finally, I asked Noah, "Who's 'I'? How come Sam became 'I'?"

"I am Sam!"

Diligently, I went through all his mistakes with him. Grammar! Spelling! Punctuation! Paragraphing! No furious foxes in Singapore! I then launched into a passionate lecture on why being able to write well was important.

Noah grimaced unrepentantly and tried to justify himself. "I don't like to write compositions because I don't want to be a typewriter when I grow up."

Well! That explains everything.

Girls and Boys

I recently read an article that said boys and girls communicate very differently. I know this to be true, just from observing my kids. April is a very intuitive communicator—she listens not just with her ears but also takes in things like body language and tone. But sometimes, it gets to the point where I can't just make any unthinking, flippant remark to April because it might get misconstrued. These days, it seems like anything can be perceived as an accusation.

For instance, our conversation might go something like this:

Me: "Have you done your homework?"
What she hears: "I hope you've done your homework."
What she says: "Not yet."

Me: "Remember to practise the sums your teacher gave you."
What she hears: "You don't practise enough."
What she says (indignantly): "I do!"

Me: "I'm not saying you don't! I'm just reminding you."
What she hears: "You always need reminding."
What she says (agitatedly): "I was going to do them later!"

Me (exasperated): "Okay fine!"
What she hears: "You're too sensitive."
What she says (muttering under her breath): "Always criticising me."

Noah is much more straightforward—he takes everything at face value. The problem is getting him to hear anything in the first place.

This is a conversation I might have with Noah, for instance:

Me: "Have you done your homework?"
What he hears: "Have you ggggnnnnnnnnnnnnnnnn."
What he says: "Mmm."

Me (louder): "Noah, have you done your homework?"
What he hears: *white noise*
What he says: Nothing.

Me (pitch rapidly rising): "Noah, if you don't do your homework, you can't play Restaurant King!"
What he hears: "Blah blah blah blah blah blah blah play Restaurant King!"
What he says (suddenly perky): "What? Can I play Restaurant King?"

Me (in Wicked Witch screech): "GO DO YOUR HOMEWORK NOW!"
What he hears (finally): "GO DO YOUR HOMEWORK NOW!"
What he says (grumbling): "Okay, okay, you don't have to shout."

In short, one hears too much, one doesn't hear enough. I'm not sure which is preferable!

Father Figure

I had to work late at the office today so I gave explicit instructions to Papa to make sure that Noah ate his dinner, took his shower and finished his homework before I got home. Imagine my frustration when I finally stepped into the house, worn out, to see Papa and Noah on the couch, watching National Geographic on TV.

"Please tell me Noah has finished his homework," I asked, silently willing it to be true.

Papa looked up with a start, rather guiltily, I thought. "Oh, err…he said he would do it after this programme."

"It's 9pm! He's supposed to be in bed by 9.30pm!" Just then, I noticed that Noah was still in his school uniform. "Don't tell me he hasn't showered!"

Papa looked sheepish. "Well, Ling, this episode is on the receding polar caps that are destroying habitats. I thought it would be educational for him."

"I don't care if it's on the nuclear missile that will obliterate the earth tomorrow! I am about to explode right now!"

"Right, right," said Papa in a conciliatory tone. "Noah, if you want to watch TV, you have to listen to Mummy, okay?"

That sparked off a fresh emission of molten lava. "What do you mean 'IF you want to watch TV'? You're supposed to listen to Mummy always!"

Fired by my ferocity, Noah scrambled to the bathroom in record time while Papa sought refuge in the bedroom.

Ohhhhh! MEN!

TERM 4

My Interpretation

I received a call from Mrs Goh. Her number appears so frequently on my phone that seeing it automatically triggers a rise in my blood pressure. What now? I'd been pretty diligent about ensuring that Noah finished his homework so it couldn't be about that.

It wasn't. This time, she complained that Noah had been handing in work that looked like kiam chye. He had a file but for some reason, he refused to use it. Instead, he had been stuffing worksheets in his bag in any old manner so that by the time they reached her, they were ripped and scrunched like some free-style papier-mâché project. Since she was on the line, she also took the opportunity to tell me that Noah was always fidgety and unable to sit still or listen in class.

I understand that she is being conscientious but honestly, I feel like teachers are slightly too gung-ho about calling parents for the smallest of misdemeanours. What does she expect me to do? Tie him down to his chair?

I don't need Mrs Goh to tell me that Noah wasn't listening. I know this first-hand. Last Thursday, he came home from school and told me he needed to cut out pictures from magazines and newspapers.

"Pictures of what?" I asked.

"Anything," he replied.

That made absolutely no sense and I knew he must have missed out part of the instructions. However, he insisted he was correct and I was in no mood to argue with him so I helped him cut out a few pictures of the glorious Swiss Alps. The next day after school, Noah told me sheepishly, "Mummy, I was wrong. I need pictures of things with flat surfaces."

It doesn't take a sleuth to figure out what happened. Basically, Noah tuned out after Mrs Goh said, "Cut out pictures of…" Hearing about the incident, Papa asked Noah whether he needed spectacles for his ears.

Noah doesn't just have a problem with selective listening, he also has a bad case of selective perception. I was quite hopeful when he told me he was third in class for the Chinese listening comprehension exam. He had scored 8/10.

Me: "You mean no one scored 10/10?"

Noah: "Have, a few got 10."

Me (nonplussed): "Huh? Then how did you get third?"

Noah: "A few got 10, some got 9. I'm the only one who got 8. One other boy got 7."

Me *facepalm*: "Alamak, so you weren't third! You were second last!!"

Noah's glass is never merely half full, it's always brimming with optimism.

Big Feet, Little Feet

I looked at April's school shoes gloomily. There was a large tear on one side, simply not mendable. It wasn't that I couldn't afford to buy her another pair, but we were less than a month away from the end of the school year and I was hoping her shoes would last till then. Alas, this was not to be. It's like hoping your final remaining piece of wrapping paper would be enough to wrap that very last Christmas present. There's a phrase for it—fat hope.

I am not being a terrible parent. I know for a fact that this is a very common occurrence in Singapore. Some primary school kids are inadvertent casualties of this phenomenon—Primary One kids drowning in super-sized uniforms (far-sighted parents in anticipation of growth spurts) and Primary Six kids in fashionably short and faded uniforms (parents reluctant to buy new ones with just a year to go).

April said one of her classmates kept tripping over her own two feet because she was wearing shoes that were two sizes too big. So clearly, pragmatism trumps dignity with Singaporean parents.

Actually, April has a pretty good record with regard to getting my money's worth when it comes to school supplies. She generally makes one pair of school shoes last at least an entire year, and they usually need to be replaced only because she has outgrown them, not because the shoes have worn out. Noah is a whole different story, wearing out five pairs of shoes in under two years. When he comes home from school, his shoes are usually in an appalling condition—scruffy and dirty. His excuse? It is hard to keep your shoes clean while playing soccer.

Likewise, I had to replace his school uniforms within a year as most of them had pen marks, thanks to the Summer debacle. To be fair, he also couldn't fit into them anymore. By the time he started Primary Two, he had grown so tubby around the middle that he could barely button his shorts without cutting off his blood circulation. In comparison, April could still wear her Primary One school uniform when she was in Primary Three. Though a little short, it was still in pristine condition.

School bags are another fast depreciating asset. Last year alone, Noah managed to rip four school bags. If April's account was right, some boys had found an ingenious way to avoid carrying their heavy bags—they just kicked the bags down the stairs. At one point, I threatened to make Noah carry his books in a plastic bag.

Anyway, I lost the gamble on April's shoes—she received spanking new school shoes over the weekend. If only there is some way of making sure they would last all through the whole of next year.

Hear Me

Noah had his English oral exam yesterday and the conversation we had when he came home from school was typical of the garbled dialogue I frequently have with him.

Me (anxiously): "So how was your oral exam?"

Noah: "Okay." (pause) "I got 7/10."

Me: "Huh? You mean you know your marks already?"

Noah: "Yes."

Me: "How did you find out?"

Noah: "Mrs Goh told me."

Me: "When did she tell you?"

Noah: "Today."

Me (frowning): "I know today. When exactly?"

Noah: "After the oral exam."

Me: "7/10 is okay, right?"

Noah: "Many people got 10/10."

Me (worried): "Really?"

Noah: "Like Zaki, Ming Hao…"

Me: "So…"

Noah: "Summer only got 9." (What does he mean 'only 9'? He got 7!)

Me (hopefully): "Did anyone get less than 7?"

Noah: "No."

Me (dead worried): "So 7/10 isn't so good…"

Noah: "Mrs Goh said my work is good."

Me: "Huh? When did she say this?"

Noah: "Today."

Me (exasperated): "I KNOW today! When exactly?"

Noah (equally exasperated): "After the oral!"

Me (puzzled): "You mean after she took you for your oral exam, she had a chat with you?"

Noah: "No, she took Ming Hao."

Me (totally confused): "She spoke to you after she took Ming Hao?"

Noah: "Hah?"

Me (frustrated): "WHAT ARE YOU TALKING ABOUT??"

Noah: "Mrs Goh didn't take me for oral! She took MING HAO."

Me: "So who took you for your oral exam?"

Noah: "I don't know her name."

Me (deep breath): "Okay, never mind. So after your oral exam, Mrs Goh spoke to you?"

Noah: "Yes."

Me: "So what did she tell you?"

Noah: "She said my work is good but if I want to get Band One, I cannot daydream."

Me: "Good."

Noah: "If I want to pull up, lah."

Me: "Pull up? Pull up your socks?"

Noah (thinking his mother's a moron): "My marks lah!"

Girl on Fire

April came home with fantastic news today. Her teacher had submitted one of her compositions for the Singapore Story Writing Competition and her entry had clinched the Best Junior Writer award!

Her story was a fictional piece on a future scenario where people had to hide underground to escape the effects of global warming. I guess her environmental fervour and all that time spent watching National Geographic with Papa paid off. The award was a big deal as the organisers had received more than 400 entries nationwide. The school would announce April's achievement during assembly and present her with a certificate.

"My teacher said I managed to bring across the impact of global warming in a touching way," commented April, beaming from ear to ear.

Noah, recalling the Earth Hour conversation, asked, "Did you write about the smelly cows?"

April ignored Noah and continued, "She wants me to try out for international writing competitions next year."

"That's super!" I gushed, delighted. "I'm so proud of you."

I gave her a giant bear hug and for once, she didn't try to squirm out of my embrace. Papa announced that the achievement called for a celebratory dinner. No meat, of course. For this occasion, I didn't mind.

Noah, peeved at all the attention April was getting, pouted. "I got 10/10 for my spelling test today."

I laughed and told him job well done. But the day really belonged to April. My daughter, the writer! A chip off the old block. I envision great things for her.

Here Wee Goh

And thus, another school year has come to an end. I'm positive Noah is relieved to have seen the last of Mrs Goh but in the end, he still managed to score Band One for both his English and Maths exams so I have to give her some credit for her teaching methods. Just for fun, I wrote a poem in honour of her, from Noah's point of view.

In Primary One, on the very first day of school,
You walked into the classroom, looking pretty and cool.
Told us your name was Miss Wee,
While smiling kindly at everybody.

English and Maths you tried to teach us.
Thirty hyper children in one class.
Very soon, you stopped smiling a lot.
Only so much patience you have got.

"Miss Wee, can I drink water?"
"Miss Wee, I can't find my eraser."
"Miss Wee, can I go toilet?"
"Miss Wee, he drew on my shirt."

When you talked, I talked too,
So what you said, I never knew.
You made me sit behind on my own.
I really didn't like to be all alone.

When I went up to Primary Two,
I thought I'd gotten rid of you.
Oh man! So sian!
You are my teacher once again.

"I'm Mrs Goh now," you say.
You got married over the holiday.
But the change is only in name.
You are still exactly the same.

"Noah, why are you dreaming?"
"Noah, didn't you learn your spelling?"
"Noah, what is 71 minus 43?"
"Noah, are you listening to me??"

I can't remember what is eight times four.
Learning times tables is such a chore.
Is it 'everybody likes' or 'everybody like' again?
Grammar is driving me insane.

Mrs Goh, why do you keep scolding me?
Don't you know I have homework allergy?
English and Maths are so boring, you see.
I only like recess and PE.

You wrote to my mother to complain,
"Noah didn't do his work again."
My mother got mad, she yelled at me,
"Another note I don't want to see!"

Your next note I hid from my mother,
So that a scolding I wouldn't get from her.
Alamak! I didn't think at all
That you would give my mother a call.

Teaching is much harder than you thought.
You must have thought of quitting an awful lot.
But still you try and try,
Even though sometimes you wonder why.

You taught us everything bit by bit.
Repeated yourself until we got it.
Addition, subtraction, multiplication,
Grammar, tenses, punctuation.

When all is said and done,
You helped me get my Band One.
So Mrs Goh, to you I say,
"Thank you for everything, you are a-okay."

Magical Mystery Tour

This year, we received a very special treat—a holiday to Tokyo! Papa's company performed well and he was given an extra month's bonus. He asked me what I wanted to spend it on and I didn't have to think twice. It had been a long time since we last went on a family holiday and with the hectic school schedules, I felt that I needed a real mental and physical break from the daily grind. Furthermore, April would be sitting for her PSLE next year and I anticipated a long, stressful year ahead, so it was a good opportunity to recharge before we turned on the academic engine at full speed.

We picked Tokyo because it fulfilled our two main criteria:

- it has great food
- it's fun

The bonus was that with budget airlines flying to Tokyo these days, air tickets were no longer horrendously expensive. The seven-hour overnight flight was largely uneventful, except that we found it difficult to sleep on the plane. So by the time we touched down at Narita Airport early in the morning, we were bleary-eyed and lethargic.

We had heard about Japanese punctuality, and we got a first taste of it with the airport limousine to the hotel. The stated pick-up time was 9.40am and I noticed that when the large digital clock hanging over the queue lane turned '9.40am', the bus cruised into our bay. Perfectly timed.

We deliberately chose a hotel close to Disneyland and Disneysea as those were the main attractions for the kids. We had planned a full day for each theme park—we were going to play till we drop!

Our first impression of Tokyo Disneyland was that it was

incredibly crowded. The sea of people that greeted us was mind-boggling, considering we were there on a weekday. I found out later that more than 30,000 people visit Tokyo Disneyland EACH DAY. No kidding.

My kids didn't care. They were like hamsters let loose in a giant field of sunflower seeds. Pirates of the Caribbean, Peter Pan, Roger Rabbit Car-Toon Spin, Snow White, Mad Hatter Tea Cups, we went on them all. Then we tried out the Haunted Mansion ride and April was a little hesitant as she was afraid it would be terrifying. I loved it! All the creaking doors, ghostly ballroom dancers and floating objects. I had to keep reassuring a spooked April next to me that it wasn't scary, but just as I was saying, "At least they don't have objects that pop out at you," we entered a graveyard scene and a head popped out of the ground!

After that, she categorically refused to go on the Splash Mountain ride which was touted as the "highest, steepest drop in Disneyland". She took one look at the log hurtling down the slide and shook her head vehemently. Of course Noah wanted to try it, so off he went with Papa.

The queues for everything were dizzying and by the time we hit the peak afternoon period, they had become a huge turn-off, with waits for rides as long as two hours. Even the queues to buy popcorn had at least 20 people in them. Absolute madness. We decided to go on the signature It's A Small World ride because the wait time was listed as five minutes.

After the ride, I griped, "There's no queue because this is the most boring ride ever!" Unless you like cutesy toys singing "It's a Small World" ad nauseum in a gazillion different languages. Or maybe I'm just a jaded old hag.

The saving grace to the crowds though, was that the Japanese were wonderfully polite people. At lunch, we went to a little pizza place that was jam-packed with bodies and limited seating. A Japanese couple saw us hovering and immediately wolfed down their food, cleared their trays and gestured for us to have the table.

We saw the same display of graciousness when we sat down along the parade route for the live show. I have honestly not met a more homogeneous or courteous people. For the show, people gathered about an hour before to find a viewing space. Every person or family that came along automatically filled up the space beside the person next to them. In perfectly ordered rows. Once a whole section was filled up, an attendant would rope up the section to signify that it was filled. Even if you got up from your seat to go to the washroom, nobody took that space. They knew it was taken.

And the best part was, during the show, nobody stood up! No jostling or shoving just to catch a glimpse of the parade. Everyone remained calmly seated, even the children, which meant we enjoyed an unobstructed view of the show. The show, by the way, was perfection—Japanese precision and technology coupled with Disney magic. It was kitschy but I loved it as much as my kids did. The Japanese embraced Disney wholeheartedly. Throughout the parks, kids, teens and even adults unabashedly donned Disney costumes, from Tigger tails and Mickey ears to full-fledged princess get-ups.

We paid a visit to Disneysea the next day and instantly found that it was much less crowded than Disneyland. I wasn't sure why because the rides were equally good, if not better, than Disneyland's. One of the highlights of Disneysea that we had been looking forward to was the Indiana Jones ride. April and Noah loved the Indiana Jones movies and just before the trip, Noah had been using pieces of string like a whip, much to the annoyance of his sister.

As we got close to the front of the line however, April started biting her nails and kept pestering me with, "Are you sure it's not scary? Are you sure there are no drops?"

We boarded a jeep which seated four in a row and went on an exhilarating ride, going through several rooms with bugs and snakes, and ending with a giant boulder rolling towards us. The jeep itself was a simulator, so it shook and bounced as if it was going through rocky terrain. Way cool!

It was an awesome ride and when the jeep emerged back into the light, I turned around to ask Noah how he liked it. To my amazement, I found his head almost in his lap—he'd closed his eyes and missed the whole thing! Alamak, full of outward bravado but actually a chicken at heart!

"The sound was very loud!" he bleated.

"Then you should have covered your ears and opened your eyes, not the other way around!"

Eager to make up for his show of weakness, he pestered me to accompany him on Flounder's Flying Fish Coaster. This was a mini roller coaster, designed for kids. He absolutely loved it and after each ride, he would plead, "Mummy, one more time! Pleeeeeeaase!!!" Because there was hardly a queue, we kept retaking the ride. We tried out the front seat, the back seat and all the ones in between. Eight times in all. By then, my back was aching from crouching in a tiny car being thrown about relentlessly, so I finally put a stop to the madness.

We stayed until the park closed so we could catch the spectacular fireworks display, the finale to an awe-inspiring water extravaganza by the lake. All in all, Disney was a huge success, and not just for the kids. Being at Disney is like being assaulted with a highly concentrated concoction of all the sunny moments you remember in your childhood, blown up 200 times and filled in with all the brilliant hues of the rainbow. It really is the happiest place on earth.

Where the Streets Have No Name

Japan is full of quirks and that's what makes it so fascinating. We had planned a trip to one of the nearby resort towns and chose to go by Shinkansen, the bullet train. The first hurdle was buying tickets when we didn't speak Japanese, but I found that a combination of basic Japanese and sign language worked.

I showed the man at the ticketing counter two fingers and gestured 'tall person'. Then, I showed him two fingers, gestured 'short person' and asked, "Ikura desuka?" Translation: two adults, two children, how much? He instantly punched out the number on a calculator and showed it to me. Tadah! Effective Communication 101.

And we were off! Right on the dot. The Shinkansen was super. Huge seats and the ride was smooooth, and of course, incredibly fast. We were seated in two rows one behind another, and an elderly gentleman, seeing that we were tourists, leapt up, stepped on a pedal right by Noah's seat and turned the front two seats to face the back two. Oh, the seats could rotate! How ingenious! I bet, though, the Japanese didn't account for little boys who wanted to turn the seat back and forth a hundred times.

When we arrived at our destination, we attempted to find our hotel which was supposed to be a six-minute walk away. Although we had a map, we still managed to get lost. I blame this on the fact that in Japan, the streets have NO NAMES. That's right. For some reason, only the very large and major roads in Japan have street names. The regular roads and small lanes (which exist in abundance in Japan) are all nameless. Apparently, when people give directions, it goes something like: "Walk 100 metres, turn right at the petrol station, walk on until you see a statue of a bear on a unicycle, then turn left."

As if this wasn't bad enough, the house/building numbers are not allocated based on their location on the street but based on the order in which they were built. Which means that house number 3 could be next to building number 41. Which could be next to house number 97. Who says the Japanese don't have a sense of humour?

We had to ask a couple of passers-by for directions to our hotel, which was challenging as we couldn't understand what they were trying to say. Nevertheless, the Japanese were so considerate and polite that even when they clearly had no clue where to go, they still tried to help us as much as they could. One lady scrutinised our map very carefully, constantly looking around the vicinity as if a neon sign would suddenly pop up and indicate the way. Then she stopped everyone who walked by to ask if they knew our desired location. At one point, our plight had attracted a small group of concerned Japanese, determined to help us poor lost tourists. Thankfully, someone finally managed to point us in the right direction.

Our hotel itself had many points of interest. One of them was the Panasonic electronic toilet with a whole side panel of buttons. We didn't know what the buttons did as they were labelled in Japanese but Noah, being the adventurous one, figured it out by trying every single one. Eventually, he emerged from the bathroom with a completely soaked shirt and announced, "I know which one squirts out water."

There was a hot spring at our hotel so we went to check it out. Since it was early in the day, it was deserted so we could fully explore the area. There were two separate bath sections, one for men, the other for ladies. Each had a common shower area where you stripped down to your birthday suit, sat on one of the stools and washed your entire body clean with soap and water. In full view of everyone.

Once you went through a sliding glass door, there was a bubbling outdoor hot bath. There, you could soak and enjoy the soothing powers of the water, as relaxed as anyone can be sitting stark naked in a public place. You could bring a towel but it was to be folded and put on top of your head (because, clearly, that was the only part of your body that needed shielding).

For such a conservative society, I am amazed that Japan has such an uninhibited practice. Having thought about taking a hot bath for all of two seconds and deciding that we were not quite so free-spirited, we went for a walk around the town.

It was about 12 degrees Celsius outside and a little drizzly, so it got rather chilly. Even though Noah was wearing quite a few layers, he kept whining about being cold so we ended up hopping into restaurants repeatedly just to be indoors. Our scenic sightseeing turned into a gastronomic adventure and we embraced it unconditionally, like true Singaporean foodies.

Most of the restaurateurs spoke no English but they were extremely warm and welcoming. Some of the menus didn't even have pictures so we had to run outside to the window display and point to the items we wanted. Udon on a blistering cold day? Heaven! Crisp and light prawn tempura with batter that melted in your mouth. Delicately sliced sashimi atop a bed of steaming white rice. Grilled slivers of beef on a hotplate. Washed down with cups and cups of ocha. Each venture out into the cold meant another epicurean delight waiting to be discovered.

We were stuffed but the low temperatures helped us burn calories, allowing us to satisfy our stomachs even more. At most restaurants, especially if they were run by elderly ladies, we would receive extra helpings or a complimentary dessert, thanks to Noah. The auntie killer charmed everyone's socks off with his dimples and cheeky grin. "Kawaii!" I heard multiple times that day. Noah didn't need to know Japanese to catch on. "They're saying I'm cute," he explained, hamming it up as April rolled her eyes.

That was the best part of our trip. Even though we eventually saw other parts of Tokyo, such as Harajuku, Shinjuku and Shibuya, the image of my family sitting without a care in the world, in a tiny restaurant tucked behind an alleyway, laughing and savouring the spread before us—that picture of true contentment is what will be seared in my memory forever.

YEAR

3

TERM 1

Always on Your Side

I always look forward to the opening of the school year, especially if the kids have been bouncing off the walls all through the six weeks of school holidays due to the accumulation of festive starch and sugars in their hyper little bodies. By the last week of the school holidays, I'll usually be counting down the number of days until they're out of my hair again.

But even before I can enjoy the peace, I'll notice something else...the silence. No sounds of bickering, of toys crashing against hard floors, of tears and childish giggles. And in a strange way, I actually miss it all.

Therein lies the contradiction—I can't wait to get the

kids out of the house and the minute they leave, I find myself waiting for them to come home. Especially when I remember that this is April's last year in primary school. I have already been warned by parents of secondary school children that they hardly get to see their kids as their school hours are even worse than those of a working adult. Mei once mused to me, "I think I've forgotten what my eldest son looks like. I never see him in daylight anymore."

I've long realised that my children will come to spend an increasing proportion of their precious growing years in school, out of my reach. My selfish desire to monopolise their time will come to nothing as their teachers, peers and friends will progressively have a far greater influence on them than I will, simply due to frequency of contact.

My pixie-faced daughter is blossoming and I can see all the signs of her quickly becoming a teenager. Noah, in my heart, will always remain my baby but I know even he is growing up fast. For this reason, I'm determined to spend more time with my kids this year, to make sure I'm a key influence in their lives. This way, even as they mature and chart their own paths, they'll know that I will always be there if they need me.

The quiet beckons. Maybe it's not so bad after all. I'll just have that cup of coffee and finish some work...only a few more hours till they're let out of school.

Class Action

The first few days of the school year are always hectic for me. Inevitably, I would be on the phone with one of these parties—the school, the Chinese tutor, the piano teacher or the school bus driver—wildly gesticulating and frantically trying to coordinate schedules that are as fickle as the stock market.

It's crazy how packed a primary school kid's timetable is these days. April brought home a note discouraging us from planning overseas trips this year as she would need to go back to school for PSLE supplementary classes during the holidays. During term time, she already has supplementary classes three times a week and CCA twice a week. This means she would be home late every weekday. I know some of her friends have tuition in every subject as well, on top of piano lessons, ballet classes and whatnot. Where do they find the time to sleep?

The Primary Three students were streamed according to their Primary Two exam results and Noah was placed in an average class this year. My hope that he would make it to the top few classes didn't materialise. I guess I shouldn't be too surprised. I'll have to make him work harder this year so he can progressively move to a better class. Everyone knows the top classes are assigned better teachers.

According to Noah, some of the boys in his previous class were in an uproar because they weren't allotted the same Primary Three class as their friends. One of them was terribly upset at being placed in the top class because none of his friends were there. He staged a protest by refusing to go to school. I guess it doesn't pay to be smarter than all your pals.

Noah's friends have been split up as well but luckily, he is still in the same class as Ming Hao. Those two are inseparable; I shudder to think what sort of tantrum Noah would have thrown if they hadn't ended up together. He is ecstatic that Summer is no longer in his class. She's in one of the top classes. Her mother should be pleased.

What's great is that Noah seems to like his form teacher this year, Miss Sharifah. From what Mei told me, she lacks experience as she's fresh from her teacher training at the National Institute of Education. However, she is very motivated and eager to make a difference. Mei is a wealth of information. I don't know how she finds out stuff like that but she's my unofficial grapevine for school news.

Noah says Miss Sharifah tells stories in class and they are always laughing. He has talked more about this teacher in the past few days than he had about Miss Wee/Mrs Goh in two years, and I take that as a good sign.

"I helped Miss Sharifah pick up her red pen and she said I'm cute," Noah declared, beaming.

"How can a teacher tell him he's cute!" April griped. "He doesn't need any more attention."

Recognising the opportunity for a motivational speech, I seized it. "If you like your teacher, Noah, you have to study hard and get good marks, then everyone will know she's a good teacher. Otherwise, God may punish you by giving you Mrs Goh again next year."

Noah looked briefly alarmed, then he relaxed. "Won't be, Mummy," he said confidently.

"Why not?"

"Mrs Goh is no longer at Somerset Primary. I think she doesn't want to teach anymore."

East Meets West

We were reminiscing about our Tokyo trip when I happened to mention that Japan was also known as the Land of the Rising Sun.

Noah: "Why is Japan called the Land of the Rising Sun?"

Me: "Well, as you know, the sun rises in the…?"

Noah: "Morning."

Me: "What? No!"

Noah: "Huh? You mean it rises at night?"

Me: "Ggggnnnnnn…the sun rises in the east!"

Noah: "Hah?"

Me (despairing): "Don't tell me you don't know the sun rises in the east and sets in the west!"

Noah: "I don't know what is east and west! Which side is east?"

Me: "East is the right side, west is the left."

Noah: "So you mean the sun rises here?" (waves right hand)

Me: "Not YOUR east! Do you think the sun rises and sets around you?"

Noah (protesting): "How would I know? I never learnt history."

Doh!

Bravissimo!

In less than a week, Noah will be sitting for his Grade Two theory exam for piano. For the most part, he's ready… except for those darn Italian terms. Most of the expressions for describing how Western classical music should be played are in Italian. Which might not be a problem for ang moh kids but for a little Chinese boy in Singapore, they may as well be in Greek. The only Italian terms Noah is familiar with are 'pizza' and 'spaghetti'.

April never liked learning the Italian terms but I don't remember her having quite so much difficulty. Part of the problem is that Noah's English is shaky to begin with. Take these Italian terms and their meanings:

Maestoso – Majestically
Brio – Vigour
Sostenuto – Sustained

Noah hasn't the faintest idea what the English words mean, let alone the Italian ones. So when learning the terms, he actually has to memorise BOTH the Italian terms and their accompanying meanings in English. Which really defeats the purpose, in my opinion.

Imagine if he comes across a piece of music which states *Sostenuto*. He won't have the slightest clue how to play that piece in a sustained manner, even if he remembers its meaning. Now if Mozart and Beethoven both spoke Singlish, things would've been so much less complicated— "Press notes longer lah!"

For example, these three terms: *Allargando*, *Allegretto*, *Accelerando* mean "broadening out", "lively, fast" and "getting faster" respectively. To Noah, they are all long words that start with the letter 'A'. Unpronounceable and indistinguishable. As with *Rallentando*, *Ritardando* and *Ritenuto*. The Italian terms that come out of his mouth are like a hysterical mix of Japanese and Tamil. His 'allegretto' sounds suspiciously like 'arigato'. The Italians would have a fit.

That's not the end of it. Mr Low had written out all the Italian terms Noah needed to know and even as he was struggling with those, I compared them with those in April's old theory book and found the latter contained at least a dozen more words. A quick check with Mr Low revealed that he had only provided the ones that were often tested. He didn't give out the full list because Noah couldn't even remember the more common ones.

Desperate times call for desperate measures. When all else fails, resort to exam skills. We're not Singaporeans for nothing! I told Noah that if the exam paper asked about an Italian term he was not familiar with, just look at the piece of music. If it looked like it had many minims and crotchets (long notes), write 'slow'. If it had many quavers and semi-quavers (short notes), write 'fast'. At least he would have a slim chance of getting it right.

Fine (The end).

Exam Fever

Yesterday, Noah sat for his theory exam and I was quite at ease as I knew he was more or less prepared for it. Mr Low was ingenious—he came up with funny phrases to help Noah remember the corresponding major and minor keys, for example:

G major + E minor = <u>G</u>iant <u>E</u>lephants
F major + D minor = <u>F</u>at <u>D</u>onkey

And Noah's personal favourite:

C major + A minor = <u>C</u>razy <u>A</u>pril

Despite knowing that Noah was ready, the morning of the exam, I suddenly experienced an irrational attack of exam anxiety and felt the urgent need to bombard him with instructions.

"Read the questions carefully."

"Check properly whether it says 'with key signature' or

'without key signature'."

"Do you have enough pencils?" I hastily packed two extra ones, in addition to the two mechanical pencils already in his pencil case.

"Make sure you write dark enough."

"But don't keep going over the notes until they're messy!"

"If you erase your work, make sure you rub it away completely."

"Take a packet of tissue in case you need to blow your nose."

"Don't draw your notes too close until they're joined together like Siamese twins."

"Don't draw your flat so round like a 'b'."

"What is *con moto*?"

This barrage continued unabated all the way to the exam centre, right to the door of the exam room.

"Remember to paste your name label on the paper."

"If you finish early, you can come out."

"But don't rush to come out! Take your time!"

"Wait for me in the corridor if I'm not here."

"If it's cold, wear your jacket."

"Do you need to go to the toilet?"

"Check your work properly!"

I was not the only restless parent. A few, after watching their kids find their seats through a small glass panel on the back door, proceeded to tap on the panel to get their kids' attention and mime last-minute instructions. It's a marvel our children are able to retain anything. I'm sure after a while, they learn to tune out our voices like white noise.

When I went to the coffeeshop to have my tea while waiting for Noah to finish his exam, I saw a grey-striped feline sprawled with wild abandon and jaunty nonchalance across a chair. It seemed to be saying, "Relax!"

And so I did. With a nice, tall glass of my favourite coffeeshop drink, teh tarik.

In Her Own Write

April is usually very guarded about letting me read her compositions. She says I'll pick them apart since I'm a journalist. Tween girls and their hyper-sensitivity! She believes I'm always looking to criticise her, which isn't true at all.

After much persuasion and promises not to be critical, she agreed to let me read a composition that she recently wrote in school:

You were out on an excursion with your class.
Your friend asked you to follow him without the teacher's permission. Based on the above situation, write a composition of at least 150 words. In your composition, make use of the points below.

- what your friend's intention was
- what happened next
- what happened in the end

Every time she comes into the classroom my ears work their magic. They completely shut out the noise. Okay, since it is science class, I shall put it in scientific terms. My ears are adapted to shut out unwanted noise. This is a behavioural adaptation. That is the best way I can put it. I have to admit that my science teacher has a special power though. That is, the power to put people to sleep just by talking.

I was brimming with excitement when I woke up. My class was about to go on an excursion to the zoo to learn about animals. At last! Something interesting in science! As we were waiting for the bus to arrive, our science teacher started briefing us about behaving well and the rules to abide by when at the zoo. I only saw moving lips, I did not hear a thing. After what seemed like ages, the excursion bus came and brought us to the zoo.

When we arrived, we headed straight for the tiger enclosure. Just then, James pulled me aside. "What?" I asked.

"Let's leave the class and go see the other animals!"

"Why? You mean we can't see them with the class?"

"Didn't you hear Mrs Lam? We do not have time to see all the animals. We are only seeing animals that adapt to extreme climates."

I debated following James. If we were found out, we would be doomed. On the other hand, I would be able to see my favourite animals like the giraffes and the crocodiles. I might even be able to write some poetry on them and I do love poetry. The choice was obvious.

James and I started walking very slowly and soon fell behind the class. Then, when our chance came, we ran off. James said I could pick whichever animal I wanted to see first, as long as I created a poem about it. I accepted the challenge.

We ran to the crocodile enclosure. "Okay, Mr Poet! What is the poem?" James asked.

"Crocodile, crocodile with your toothy grin. With your cunning smile and your scaly chin," I answered.

"Only two lines?"

"It's called a couplet."

"I think it's lame. But it's still a poem anyway, I guess."

Victory! I won the challenge! For the rest of the day, James and I saw many cool animals and Mrs Lam was not in sight. In the end, we headed back towards the exit. We planned to hide behind the vending machine and wait to rejoin the class. This way, we would be twenty minutes ahead of the class which would only arrive at one o'clock.

However, much to our surprise, the entire class was already there. So was Mrs Lam. She caught sight of us and stormed over. "Where were you two? You don't know how worried we were! When we did a headcount and found out you two were missing, we traced back our steps and even searched the gents! We came here to see if you were at the fast food restaurant!"

Amazingly, my ears could not work their magic this time so I got it at full blast about safety and causing inconvenience to others. With Mrs Lam shouting at the top of her lungs, I was surprised she did not get a sore throat. I wondered why. However, I guess there will never be a scientific explanation for that.

April scored 37/40 for the composition and I felt the high marks were well deserved. I was not sure what to expect but it wasn't this. My editor told me that some schools teach students to memorise and regurgitate a multitude of "good phrases" that make children's writing so unnatural. It's like someone trying to squeeze in as many bombastic words within each sentence as possible, for the sole reason of demonstrating sophisticated vocabulary. It makes for very dreary reading, like ploughing through a comprehension passage.

April didn't do anything like that. Her language was simple but fluid, and I was amazed that her story didn't have a complex plot, yet was interesting to read. Considering the time constraints, it was a great effort. I was delighted that her teacher recognised the value of her style and I hoped the PSLE examiners would too.

Gratified that I didn't have to feign admiration, I turned to April and smiled. "I love it! It's very good."

To my exasperation, April replied, "You're just saying that because I said you couldn't criticise! You really hate it!" She snatched the exercise book from my hands and ran to her room.

Ohhhh! There's no pleasing this girl!

Twisted Logic

Noah has been learning to play badminton since the beginning of this year as part of being in the Fitness Club. As with most sports, he enjoys playing the game and picked up the skills relatively quickly. However, as is common among many young kids, Noah hates to lose. Sometimes, he would come home from the Fitness Club in a huff, terribly upset because he had lost a game to another schoolmate.

I had to constantly remind him that he needed to be persistent and not accept failure so easily. When he became frustrated, he made even more mistakes. I told him he should just focus on one point at a time and keep trying.

Yesterday, this lesson was hammered home as Noah excitedly recounted to me his performance against another student in a five-point round game. He was down 0-2 and his opponent needed only one more point to win the round. Coming from behind, Noah took the next three points and won the round, to the dismay of his opponent.

I thought this was the perfect opportunity to reinforce the message I'd been trying to convey to him.

Me: "Excellent job! So now you know what's important in a game?"

Noah (promptly): "Footwork."

Me: "Huh? No!"

Noah: "Smashing?"

Me (facepalm): "You were two down and you still managed to win. So what did you learn from that episode?"

Noah (light bulb): " Not to get frustrated."

Me: "That's right. Of course footwork is important. But more importantly, you must never…?"

Noah: "Lose."

Me: "GAHHHH!!"

Noah (catching on like a game show contestant): "Give

up! I mustn't give up!"

I'm sure, eventually, he will learn how to give me all the answers I want to hear but it's clear that for little Noah-poleon Bonaparte, all he cares about is winning.

TERM 2

Twelve Candles

This year I decided to let April have a birthday party since it's the last year she would be with her primary school classmates. She requested a sleepover as a special treat and I acquiesced since she had been reasonably diligent in her studies. I even allowed her to cancel one Chinese tuition session.

She printed out her own invitation cards, created little flowers from coloured tissue as party gifts, and even baked cookies for her friends. I borrowed a couple of extra mattresses from Grandma to accommodate all eight girls in April's room.

Right from the start, I was quite relaxed, unlike for

Noah's party last year. Organising a girls' party is a walk in the park compared to a boys' party (which is like trying to run 5 kilometres while juggling.)

The girls arrived, checked out April's books and toys, and then just SAT AROUND CHATTING. No jumping, fighting or screaming. I overheard snippets of their conversations. Apart from the usual gossip about teachers and friends, there was also the occasional "Do you think Mark likes her?" followed by an outbreak of whispers and giggles. Double confirmed. Puberty has arrived.

Dinner was at the table where the girls ate fried rice, grilled chicken and soup, like civilised human beings. How is it that one little chromosome can make such a difference in behaviour?

I had told Noah not to disrupt the party but the busybody couldn't restrain his curiosity and slunk into April's room to find out what everyone was doing. After he was unceremoniously yelled at by his sister to get lost, he took revenge by standing outside her door and launching several toy cars into her room using a rubber band catapult.

"MUMMMYYYY!!! Tell this pest to stop disturbing us!"

I then decided it would be less trouble all around to give Noah a free pass to play computer games, so that there would be no more interruptions. That evening though, when he could hear the girls laughing and talking in April's room, he felt rather put out at not being included in the fun.

"Girls are so noisy," he told me indignantly, as he struggled to find the right word. "They're so...so...inconvenient."

I tried not to smile. "Do you mean inconsiderate?"

"Yes, that too."

The girls chatted through the night. I don't think they got much sleep. In the morning when I peeked into the room, they were all out like a light. Breakfast was more like brunch since it was 10.30am before the first girl started to rouse. As they tucked into their egg sandwiches and pancakes, I could see from the girls' happy faces that the party was an unqualified success.

After her friends had left and I was clearing the dishes, April suddenly ran up to me and gave me a hug. "Thank you for the party, Mummy," she said shyly. I was touched. It was so rare for me to receive a spontaneous gesture of affection from April. It was like a gift.

Happy birthday, my darling girl.

Tech Talk

It's hard keeping up with technology. Just when I had finally set up a Facebook account, I was told I needed Twitter. There's also Instagram, Tumblr and a million other things that I've never heard of because I'm a tortoise in the age of the nuclear-powered hare.

We don't even give email a second thought now. How did we ever communicate before? Phone? Memos? Yes, when I first started work, we typed out memos! And 'cc' actually meant giving someone a physical copy!

It was only when I helped Noah open an email account that I remembered how momentous email was, like getting a key to your very own personal letter box. He was terribly excited about it and sent me his debut email:

Dar mummy I lik having an mail. Now I can snd mails to my frinds. lov noah

Besides realising that I had forgotten to teach Noah to use the 'Enter' button, I was appalled by his atrocious spelling and chided him for it.

"I know how to spell!" he protested. "There's no 'e'!"

"What on earth are you talking about? Of course there is an 'e' on the keyboard!"

He looked down at the keyboard. "I can't find it."

"You silly, it's th…oh." The 'e' had been typed on so frequently that the letter had completely worn off the key.

At first, Noah didn't quite understand that he was unlikely to get any new mail if he didn't tell anyone what his email address was, which he kept confusing with his password. I had told him to keep his password a secret from everyone except me, the sole guardian, so he would whisper conspiratorially to me, "Mummy, I typed 'Ultimatebigchillnoah' but it doesn't work."

"That's your username, silly."

It didn't help that he insisted on having such a long

username and he kept entering it wrongly, thanks to his keyboard-challenged typing and spelling skills.

When I was at work today, I received this email from Noah:

Dear mummy
Are you busy?
Love noah

My reply:

Dearest Noah,
Yes I am.
Love, Mummy

After 10 minutes:

Dear mummy
Very busy?
Love noah

My reply:

Yes!!

After 15 minutes:

Dear mummy
Good luck on your work.
Love noah

My reply:

Thank you, Noah. Now can you please go do your homework instead of writing emails?
Love, Mummy

After 20 minutes:

Dear mummy
OK. I love you.
Love noah

I don't care if I'm a sucker. I have the sweetest son.

Out of Our Heads

Today I had lunch with Mei at a café near Somerset Primary. The coffee was surprisingly first-rate and not too pricey as well. I suppose the establishment wants to milk all the caffeine-addicted teenagers from the schools close by. Kids have too much pocket money these days.

As we were sharing a slice of chocolate fudge cake, Mei casually asked how Noah did in his English presentation. I must have looked like a mighty idiot because my jaw dropped and I asked, bewildered, "What English presentation?"

Apparently, the kids were supposed to prepare a two-minute presentation of the person they most admired in their lives. They would be scored on presentation skills and the marks would count towards the SA1.

I told Mei, despairingly, that Noah hadn't breathed a word of this to me and I was hearing it for the first time. What I like about Mei is that she doesn't judge me. She's always sympathetic and she understands my predicament because Ming Hao is her youngest of three boys and he is as nonchalant about studies as Noah.

"Don't worry, Ling," she said reassuringly. "Noah is a resourceful boy. I'm sure he did just fine."

However, she triggered another anxiety attack when she shared that she and her husband sat down after dinner every night to revise lessons with their kids, conscientiously going through what had been taught in school that day. Gosh, I was about to hyperventilate.

Is that what other parents do to help their children? I envy Mei for having a husband who is so involved in their children's studies. I can't imagine Papa doing the same. His idea of contributing to our kids' education is to make them watch the migration of Christmas Island red crabs on National Geographic. Maybe WE should consider migrating. To a country where there is no PSLE or SA1.

Feeling terribly guilty about being a Slacker Mum, I went into Super Mum mode that evening. In the space of two hours after dinner, I reviewed Noah's spelling words with him, set a Maths paper for April, coached Noah in oral, marked April's paper, and went through it with her.

There was a lot of yelling (will I never see the end of those careless Maths mistakes?) and lots of tears. I was mentally and physically exhausted, and about to go to bed early when I remembered the English presentation.

I grilled Noah. "Why didn't you tell me about it?"

Noah hung his head. "I forgot."

"How could you forget something like that? It's counted in your exam! So what did you say in the end?"

"I just went up and said the person I admire most is my sister because she's in Primary Six and she's very smart and she can write very well and she can talk very fast and she can punch like a boy."

I was slightly taken aback. The person Noah admires most is April? This was news to me, considering they fought so much.

"So what did Miss Sharifah say?"

"She said it's good because I can speak loudly. Some people talk so softly nobody can hear. She gave me 8/10. That's good, you know. Some people only got 5/10."

I was relieved. Basically he went up, winged it and came through. As I lay in bed, I wondered if maybe my methods for Noah were wrong after all. It seems like when he is left to his own devices, he somehow manages to get by. Unfortunately, I don't have the courage to test if that theory is correct.

For Your Entertainment

Since the composition fiasco with Noah last year, I haven't revisited compositions with him. I don't relish going through the process of forcing him to write. It's too much of an effort and I tell myself that it doesn't help much anyway. Call me an ostrich but the real reason is probably because I don't want to come to terms with the fact that his standard of English is pretty awful.

I was, therefore, pleasantly surprised when I came across this composition in his bag, that he had written in school:

"Hurray! Hurray!" "The exams are over!" the students at Sunshine school shouted. Mary was so happy that the exams were over. She was so proud of herself because she got full marks for all subjects. Mary rushed back home.

When she was on her way home, she thought, "Mum will be so proud of me, I can't wait to get home." When Mary was walking along her corridor, she noticed a man acting suspiciously. "Oh no, the strange man is trying to break into my neighbour's house! I must warn Mum quickly."

Mary quickly and quitely went into her house and immediatly ran strait to her mother. "Mum! Mum! I saw a man trying to break into our neighbours house!" she said. "Oh no, quick, we must call the police at once!" Mum replied. Mary nodded and rang the police.

By the time the man was coming out of the house, the police were here. The police caught the man red-handed.

The man mumbled, "The police are here, I'm done for!"

The man tried to run as fast as he could, but the police caught up with him. The police pulled the man down to the ground and handcuffed him.

"Wait! I can explain, OW!"

The police ignored the man and took him to the police station.

Mary's mother was indeed proud of Mary. Her mother praised Mary for being vigilant. Mum gave her thumbs up and hugged her. Mary was so happy because she did a good deed by staying alert.

There were quite a few spelling and grammatical errors but on the whole, it had good development and was a coherent story. It was a vast improvement from his earlier attempt and I rather enjoyed reading it because his use of dialogue was so animated it made me laugh.

I told Noah it was an excellent effort and asked, "Where did you learn the phrase 'being vigilant'? Must be from reading books. Told you it's important to read."

"No, I heard it on TV." Noah turned to me and said, without missing a beat, "You should let me watch more TV."

Doh.

Feels Like Home(work)

One thing I've come to notice about Noah is that he lacks tenacity and that's not good. When he's unable to do a piece of homework or encounters difficulties, he quickly gets frustrated and gives up. I often have to spend time calming him down and giving him a pep talk just so I can get him to re-focus on the problem.

I'm not sure if this has anything to do with being the younger child, who has always had his older sister pave the way for him. After the English presentation, I now know that despite his squabbles with April, deep down, he enjoys having an older sister. I overheard him telling some of his friends, "My sister is in Primary Six" with great pride, for no other reason than the fact that she was three whole years older than any of them.

I didn't realise just how much he had come to rely on her until yesterday. He brought home a list of words which were scrambled. He was supposed to unscramble them to reveal a series of words but he couldn't solve the last two. Ming Hao obviously faced the same problem because he rang Noah for help. I was by the phone when he called and was not very pleased to hear Noah say, "I haven't done it because my sister isn't home yet."

After Noah had hung up, I launched into a "What-do-you-mean-your-sister-is-not-home-so-you-can't-do-your-homework?" and "Why-does-she-have-to-do-your-homework-for-you?" lecture.

"But I already tried and I can't do it!" By trying, he meant that he had stared at the letters for a good 10 seconds and no word had magically formed in his head.

"You have to put in more effort and not give up!" I

insisted. I took out the Scrabble board and made him slowly try to rearrange the given letters in the first word. I had to grit my teeth through a loud and discordant five minutes of "I don't know! I can't do it!" before he suddenly grinned and told me he'd solved it—CINEMA.

For the second word, I figured that there was a missing letter. Alamak, can't even copy correctly. I told Noah so but he wouldn't believe me and we went into another Battle of the Stubborn People: "It's wrong!" "No, it's not!" "You copied wrongly!" "No, I didn't!" Stamping of feet. In the end, he agreed to call Ming Hao to check. When he got off the phone, he told me, sheepishly, "I missed out the N. The answer is CEILING."

I don't know if this episode has taught him a lesson about perseverance. Maybe I should engrave Bob the Builder's slogan "Yes We Can!" on all his stationery.

Mamma Mia

I think it's a cruel joke that Mother's Day falls right smack in the middle of SA1. How can I celebrate and relax when I'm stressed out over exams and knee deep in assessment papers? Papa reminded me that Mother's Day originated from the US and offered to take over revision with the kids for the day. Now, THAT'S a super Mother's Day gift! If only I can persuade him to do this on a regular basis.

My kids were very sweet. April woke up early to make

me a breakfast of ham and scrambled eggs, and presented me with a homemade card using scrapbooking material. At first, I was puzzled when Noah thrust a tissue box into my arms. A tissue box? Ah, but it wasn't just any old tissue box. He'd filled it with little scraps of paper, each with a scribbled picture of a pair of hands or lips.

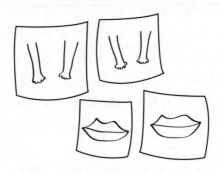

He explained that anytime I felt like it, I could draw out a piece of paper and if it showed hands, I would get a hug from him. If it showed lips, I would get a kiss. The best part? He assured me the gift would never expire. Sweetness overload.

That wasn't all. He had clipped two $2 notes to the side of the box and scrawled: "This is your first allowance from your son!"

That made me chuckle. Four whole dollars! Well, if you calculate its value from an eight-year-old's perspective, it's probably closer to $400. Quite a fortune, really. I'm considering framing the notes.

Some time back while I was sitting in Noah's room

watching him play, he suddenly turned to me, gave me a bear hug and said, "You're the best mummy in the world."

Mother's Day is grand and I appreciate the wonderful gestures of love. But what are even better are displays of affection in an otherwise ordinary moment, without the motivation of a dedicated day or event. These are the little sparks that remind me, especially during times of self-doubt or reproach, that I must have at least done something right.

Armageddon

I am totally devoid of stamina after having partaken in the SA1 exam race with April and Noah over the past two weeks. Of course I was an active participant! I believe in compensating my kids' bochap-ness with my kancheong-ness. If the Exam Gods see my panicky state, they might pity me enough to bestow better grades on my happy-go-lucky kids.

I thought Noah's overall results were okay but they could have been better. Looking at his Science paper gave me a lot of angst. Several questions that he had answered incorrectly baffled me as I'd gone through the concepts with him several times. For one multiple choice question, he knew the correct answer but marked the wrong number.

"Why are you throwing away marks?" I wailed, extremely agitated. I added up all the marks that I deemed he SHOULD have gotten had he been more careful/focused/

awake and announced very loudly to him, "YOU GAVE AWAY EIGHT MARKS!!"

April topped her class in English, and did well in all other subjects except Maths, which let her down again. When I saw a mistake she had made on her Maths paper: 8/100 = 4/25, I had an apoplectic fit.

"How can you make 'this sort of careless mistake?" I yelled. "It's only three months to the prelims and then the PSLE. You're still making mistakes like this?"

"Nothing I do is ever good enough!" she retorted. "I already tried my best!"

"This can't be your best. If you had tried your best, you wouldn't have made this mistake. This is not acceptable."

"That's only one mistake! The rest of the paper wasn't so bad."

"In the PSLE, every mark counts and you know that! One mark can mean the difference between an A and an A*. Do you want to do badly and end up in some neighbourhood secondary school?"

"What's wrong with that?" she snapped. "Maybe it's better that I go to a neighbourhood school, then you won't pressurise me so much."

"How dare you talk back to me?" I smouldered. "You have such a bright future and you want to throw it all away because you didn't focus enough not to make careless mistakes?"

"Maybe I'm not that smart!" She looked deflated and

started to cry. "I really did try my best." She ran to her room and didn't come out for dinner.

It's been a horrible day. I don't know what to say to April or how to motivate her anymore.

TERM 3

What If

April worked really hard during the June holidays, dutifully attending all her supplementary classes and completing the extra work that her teachers doled out. I said no more about the blow up we had. We need to look forward, not back. I also decided to put her piano lessons on hold since it's only a few more months before the plague of the PSLE is over. We should focus our efforts on overcoming this hurdle, then we can relax.

I keep saying 'we'. I wonder if the Ministry of Education knows that the PSLE is as tough on parents as it is on the children?

During the holidays, April also worked on a piece for

the International Environment Council's Writing Competition. Her teacher felt that this was right up April's alley, what with her passion for environmental issues. It's a very prestigious competition. The organisers receive thousands of entries each year and the winners are featured in their magazines which have a massive worldwide circulation.

Over the past year, April has developed a deep love of poetry and she decided to send in a poem instead of an essay. She worked on it for a whole week, until I was nervous that it would eat into her revision time. I didn't say anything though because I didn't want to trigger another outburst. In the end, I'm glad I didn't because what she came up with truly communicated her conviction.

What if...
Humans didn't ever exist?
I think the earth would probably flourish
All.of this man-made machinery
Would be replaced by lush greenery
Where there are factories, cars
And streets of hot melting tar
Would be forests, flowerbeds
And thriving animals instead

What if...
All of nature could talk, scream and shout?
Only then, might we understand
That all this hunting we could do without
As the blood of these animals stain the land
All the felled trees would lie there groaning

The sky, filled with toxic air, would be choking
Mother Nature, is honestly going to die
But why won't you stop this, why won't you try

Who cares?
Well you're a fine one to speak
But even now, surely you feel the heat
The earth's heating up, the icecaps are melting
A few years on, the heat will be sweltering
Some countries will flood as sea levels rise
If you own beach houses say your goodbyes
But in other countries, there is no water about
It's the opposite of a flood, it's a drought!

So what?
Haven't you been listening all this time?
Don't you understand the severity of this?
To ignore this would be a serious crime
As this problem is too apparent to dismiss
Entire ecosystems are dying
Why aren't you even trying?
To save your own home and life
As well as your dear children and wife

Oh no!
Oh yes! Don't you hear the anxiety in my voice?
My heart breaks when I see what we've done
Your own life's at stake, you've got no choice
It is your duty and from it, please don't shun
Don't think "But soon, I'll be dead and gone
It won't affect me; I'll carry just carry on

With my own work and my own business"
'Cause then, your children will inherit this mess

But, but…
Your business in fossil fuels will have to fold?
Well, that's a price you'll have to pay
Earth's call of help can't be put on hold
Please respond to it, don't turn her away
All this that I have said is true
The earth's in a sorry state
Do your part now, I implore you
Before it truly is too late

But how?
Well, I am so glad you asked
Since saving the world isn't an easy task
But do things bit by bit and start small
And you'll help the earth in no time at all
By just recycling a ton of paper
You save 380 gallons of oil and 17 trees
As well as 7,000 gallons of water
And 4,000 kilowatts of energy

That's amazing!
I'll say! And you don't have to stop there
You can also help spread awareness across the nation
Maybe by starting an earth-saving trend somewhere
Or even better, join an environmental organisation

So you see you don't need superpowers to save the earth
But the effort you put in will be of immeasurable worth
For even though we live in different places

Or are of many unique, special races
When we all unite just for this one cause
We'll accomplish things worthy of Mother Nature's
applause

April shows such maturity in her writing. I'm very impressed. I wonder where she learnt to write like that because I couldn't have written anything remotely close to this at her age. I'm so incredibly proud of her.

Saya Boleh! I Can!

The other day in the car, we saw some Malay teenagers dressed in their best baju for Hari Raya, in cheery and matching hues. Noah asked where they were going and Papa said, "They're probably going to visit their cikgu."

Noah immediately piped up, "I thought cikgu is a fruit."

Me (exasperated): "That's CHIKU! Cikgu means teacher."

That reminded me of the Conversational Malay enrichment programme that Noah had taken in school for the first six months of this year. The course aimed to reinforce the multi-racial environment in Singapore, meaning that Malay and Indian pupils had to learn Mandarin while Chinese kids learnt Malay.

Noah handed me a school flyer stating that he had completed the beginners' module of 20 hours. I thought, "Oh, that's terrific. He now knows some basic Malay."

Me: "So what have you learnt from the class?"

Noah: "Err…"

Me (frowning): "You had so many sessions, you must have learnt something!"

Noah: "I can say 'My name is Noah'."

Me: "How?"

Noah (slowly): "Nama saya Noah."

Me: "Okay, what else? Can you count to 10?"

Noah (looking blank): "Umm…"

Me: "Oh, for Pete's sake…"

Noah (protesting): "It's not my fault! I didn't have the textbook."

Me: "Huh? What textbook?"

I read the flyer carefully again. Darn it! He was supposed to have bought a textbook. How did I miss that? "Well, you could have asked me for the money. You mean you went six months without the textbook and didn't say anything?"

Noah: "The teacher said those who don't have can share."

Me: "Okay, but 20 sessions, surely you must have learnt something."

Noah (thinking hard): "I can say 'Good morning, teacher'."

Me: "That doesn't count! You use that all the time to greet your Malay teachers. I want to know what you learnt from the class."

Noah (brightening up): "I know what 'class' is in Malay."

Me: "What?"

Noah: "Kelas."

All I can say is, thank goodness Conversational Malay is not an examinable subject.

To 'Cher with Love

This year was the first time that I didn't dread going to Noah's Parent-Teacher Conference and it's all thanks to Miss Sharifah. She's always kind, never writing "Can do better!" or "Try harder!" on his worksheets. Instead, she writes "Good job!" and pastes smiley stickers. On the papers that he doesn't do so well in, she at least writes "Good try!" or "Keep going!"

Teachers don't realise how far a little encouragement can go, especially for young kids. Noah's attitude has improved significantly this year. Even though his work is still far from exemplary, at least he listens better in class and I give Miss Sharifah all the credit. I know teaching Noah is no picnic as he can be very trying, so I appreciate her even more for it.

In person, Miss Sharifah was everything I imagined her to be. She had a sunny nature with a sparkle in her eye and she clearly loved children. She was very animated when she spoke and she laughed a lot. I could see why Noah liked her.

"Mrs Tan, Noah is very adorable and he loves stories," she shared. "Sometimes, he talks a little too much but that's just part of his personality. He's a very sociable boy and I try to turn that into something that would benefit the class, by making him help a weaker student in Maths, for example. He's always ready to help others. He's great that way."

Finally, a teacher who understood my son and accepted him for who he was! I wanted to adopt her as Noah's permanent teacher. Back home, I realised that Miss Sharifah's impact on Noah was even greater than I had thought when he actually showed empathy for the difficulty of her job.

Noah: "Miss Sharifah works very hard."

Me: "Why do you say that?"

Noah: "Because there are 44 pupils in the class and it's mostly boys."

Me: "Why is it harder to teach boys?"

Noah (making a face): "You know why."

Me (amused): "I don't know, you tell me."

Noah: "We talk and play all the time."

Me: "So you're one of them."

Noah: "Yeeesss…"

Me: "That's not nice. Since she's kind to you, you should pay attention and listen to her."

Noah: "I know." (pause) "It's August already."

Me: "That's right."

Noah: "When the teacher is nice, time goes by very quickly!"

Winner Takes It All

Today was a gift of a day. April came home, her face glowing with euphoria. "Mummy, Mummy, I won the writing competition!"

The details came tumbling out in a jubilant jumble: She had clinched the medal for Best Young Writer in the International Environment Council Writing Competition. There were only two Singaporeans among the winners. Her poem would be published in the organiser's quarterly magazine. A newspaper reporter came to school to interview her today on her win.

It was almost too much to absorb. Could this really be happening to April? Seemed like a dream but there she was jabbering away, giddy with happiness. My heart was so full of pride I felt like I was about to burst.

That was not all. April also did spectacularly well in her prelims, coming in third in the whole Primary Six level at Somerset Primary. Her indicative T-score was 259—a fantastic achievement. With a score like that, she could easily get into a top school.

How much good news could one take in a day? I was over the moon. "April, very well done!" I praised. "Okay, if you score 260 and above for the PSLE, I'll buy you an iPhone."

April shrieked with excitement, "Thank you, Mummy! I'll try, I really will."

When Papa heard about my promise of a reward, he

expressed doubt. "Are you sure we should be rewarding good results with material things, Ling? Aren't we sending the wrong message?"

"At least I'm trying to do something to motivate her!" I said, irate. "What's your contribution?"

"Alright, alright," he hurriedly conceded. "You know best."

Trust Papa to pour cold water on my efforts. Giving April an incentive would motivate her to push herself even harder. Just a few more months to go; I can't have her slacken her pace now. Everything is coming together nicely.

The Long and Winding Road

This is it—the final stretch to the PSLE. It's just two weeks to the first paper and exactly three weeks till it's all over. It has been a very draining process and I feel like I've been running a marathon next to April. To make matters worse, she has developed eczema on her arms and neck. I told her to stop pawing at her skin as it aggravates the condition but she said it itches like crazy. I took her to the doctor and he diagnosed it as stress-induced. This PSLE is getting under her skin, literally.

I can sympathise. It seems like the entire community of school, teachers, parents and kids has been blasted with a wave of mutually reinforcing kancheong-ness. From the start of this term, it has been intensive revision every day, with remedial sessions added. April has been coming home with as many as four PSLE papers a day, one for each subject, as homework. The next day, she would hand them all in and exchange them for another set. I think it's especially hectic for her class because the school wants to try and produce another top PSLE student. April told me that some of her friends' parents were adding to the workload by sending their children for intensive tuition classes and boot camps.

It's not just the parents and the teachers; many of April's friends are pushing themselves at this breakneck pace. April has been ultra-conscientious, working out her own revision timetable. Yesterday, I took a peek at her timetable and I was just floored:

<u>Monday</u>: Homework Shower Chinese revision Dinner Maths Revision

<u>Tuesday</u>: Homework Shower English Oral practice Dinner Science Revision

<u>Wednesday</u>: Homework Shower English Compo revision Dinner Chinese Oral Maths Revision

<u>Thursday</u>: Homework Shower Chinese Oral practice Dinner Maths Revision

<u>Friday</u>: Homework Shower Chinese revision Dinner Science Revision

<u>Saturday</u>: Chinese tuition Do papers for every subject!!

<u>Sunday</u>: Chinese tuition homework Revise every subject!!

There was even a post-it with a self-motivation note on her desk: "iPhone! i can do it!"

She has barely taken a break and has been going to bed later and later, which I don't approve of. I've always been the one pushing April to work harder but even I wonder if it's all a little too much, too intense. She is beginning to look mentally saturated and weary, and I am worried that she'll be burnt out right before the PSLE.

So today, on impulse, I did something very uncharacteristic. I told April to drop everything and just relax for the day. She was suspicious at first and a little reluctant but when she saw that I meant it, I think she was secretly relieved. She played computer games, watched TV and read her favourite books all afternoon—a taste of what post-PSLE life would be like. Tomorrow, she'll be back at her books but it was good to see the worry lines on her forehead disappear for a while.

Beautiful Boy

Last month, I was sharing my woes on Noah's schoolwork and behaviour with my editor when he commented, "It must be very difficult to have a sister like April."

When I asked him what he meant, he explained that growing up, he had always felt inferior to his older brother who did well in school, was a star sportsman and a popular leader. He had lived in his brother's shadow for years, especially since his parents always compared him to his brother.

"But Boss, I don't compare my kids," I protested. "I make it a point not to do so because they're so different."

"Ling, you don't have to," he said. "From your different treatment of them, they will know. Most kids are smart enough to know how they measure up in their parents' eyes."

I thought about what he said. It was true that each time April bagged some sort of achievement, like the International Environment Council medal, Noah became abnormally quiet. It probably doesn't help that in our family, accomplishments are heavily weighted towards April, not Noah, especially academically.

Noah tends to be at the receiving end of my wrath also because he's less compliant. His schoolwork see-saws depending on whether he's particularly inspired at the time he's doing it. It sometimes takes several repetitions before he can grasp a concept and he often forgets what he has learnt. When the going gets tough, he loses interest, makes excuses or cries.

It's hard to maintain a positive attitude towards kids who constantly don't conform. Even though I've probably read a thousand times that positive strokes work better than negative ones, yelling comes instinctively to me. I suspect it's in my DNA.

There were periods this year when Noah seemed forlorn and subdued, almost lost. It felt like he was going through the daily motions aimlessly, getting into trouble or throwing tantrums without being able to explain why. It got to a point where I felt sorry for him; he was like a lost lamb. Remembering what my editor said, I figured that maybe what Noah needed was an affirmation of his self-worth and when I tucked him in bed one night, in addition to the usual hugs and kisses, I told him, "You're a good boy."

Every night since then, I started telling him, "You're a good boy." I don't know if it's my imagination but it seems like Noah has started becoming more sensible. He fusses less about doing his homework and actually practises the piano on his own. Now when he receives a sub-par mark for spelling or a test, there is no need to scold him because he is visibly dissatisfied with his own result. Last week, he had so much homework that it cut into his play time but he told me he wasn't complaining because he knew the exams were coming up. (Of course he had to advertise it to me! A sacrifice is not a sacrifice unless someone knows about it.)

I can't be sure but perhaps the words of affirmation have encouraged and motivated him somewhat. Maybe hearing that he is a good boy every night has, in some small part, helped him realise that his scrapes and misdemeanours don't define who he is.

I've known all along that Noah is a good boy at heart. He just needed to believe it too.

TERM 4

Please Stop Learning Everything

It's here—PSLE week. This is what April has been working towards. Everything now rests on these next few days.

Day 1: English
Uneventful. April found the paper to be a breeze. She wrote five pages for the composition. How she managed to do that within one hour, I have no idea.

Day 2: Maths
April came home in tears, declaring it an unequivocal disaster. She said that when she saw how difficult some of the questions were, her brain just shut down and she couldn't focus on the paper.

"Did you still try every sum?" I asked concerned. "You didn't leave any question blank, did you?"

"Yeesss…but I think I got many of them wrong."

I told her it was okay, not to be upset and to concentrate on the upcoming papers. I was sure it wasn't as bad as all that, she had so much practice. She was just being her perfectionist self. It is normal to feel let down when you've invested so much effort and then you mess up, even a little. In my head, I wondered if she could still get her A* though. It would be such a waste if she missed out on that.

Day 3: Chinese

Hooray! April was most worried about the composition because she was afraid that she wouldn't understand the given topic. Instead, the topic was a car accident, something she had written about a thousand times before. She had memorised lots of good phrases for this topic so she could essentially regurgitate everything into one composition.

She also found the main paper reasonably easy. The Chinese tutor would be pleased.

Day 4: Science

April told me she wasn't sure about the lizard question. At least she could identify the solar panels. Her friend thought it was a windmill on a plastic bottle.

That was all she would say because this was her last PSLE paper! She threw her bag down and announced to me, "Don't ask me anymore how it went, I don't care. I'm freeeee!!"

I knew exactly how she felt. It was like in *The Lord of the Rings* when Frodo finally threw the ring into the Fire of Mount Doom and declared, "It is done!" It is done indeed. I have visions of George Michael belting out "Freedom!" in my head.

Now there's nothing left for April to do except to wait for the results. I plan to take her out for a celebratory ice cream cone but I'll have to rush home because I still have to help Noah revise for his SA2. A mother's job is never done.

Science Fiction

I find Science in primary school extremely strange. The subject is introduced in Primary Three with textbooks that read very simply and come complete with lovely pictures, like kids' National Geographic magazines. But just studying the textbooks is to guarantee failure. Some of the questions in the Science exam papers are ridiculously tough and tricky.

In addition, a good grasp of the English language is required to fully comprehend the questions. This is where Noah often runs into trouble. There was a question in his Science exam paper: "Draw two conclusions from the experiment above."

I was vexed when I saw that Noah had left the answer space blank. "How could you have missed out this two-mark question?"

Noah explained huffily, "I didn't know how to draw

the answer!"

Sometimes, it's his odd perspective that trips him up. This was another question:

> Mr Cheng brought a mystery animal to class and asked his pupils to guess what it was. The clues are listed below:
>
> - This animal is covered with fur.
> - This animal eats meat and bone.
> - This animal can run and jump on land.
> - This animal can swim in water.
> - This animal can be kept as a pet.
>
> Name the mystery animal.

I didn't see what the big mystery was. I mean, it was quite obviously a dog. However, Noah wrote: "The mystery animal is a platypus."

I wailed in despair, "How on earth can it be a platypus??"

"I didn't know a dog could swim!"

"It's a pet! How can a platypus be a pet?"

"I thought you could keep it in a tank."

He better not get any ideas. I have enough nightmares of his frog doing a Houdini from the tank as it is.

Good is Good

It's the last day of school and Noah brought back his report book. His results were a mixed bag but it's becoming clear to me that quite unlike his sister, his strength is in Maths, with Science a close second. His English is mediocre and his

Chinese is scraping the bottom of the barrel. Languages are not his strong suit. Moving ahead, I'll need to double the effort to make sure he keeps up with English and Chinese so his grades don't slip further.

The system of streaming the children every year is so unhealthy and adds to the ugly competitive spirit. It means that it isn't enough for Noah to do well; I need him to do better than the other kids in his class so that he can be promoted to a reasonable class next year. When he told me a few days ago that he had scored 94/100 for Maths, I was initially delighted, then concerned when I found out that many of his classmates had scored over 90, indicating that it was a simple paper.

Ming Hao had barely passed his Maths exam for the SA1 and made a huge improvement to score 80 at the SA2. When I spoke to Mei, she laughed sheepishly and admitted, "I was still thinking, how come he couldn't get Band One."

It struck me that we Singaporean parents are hard to please.

Noah has long learnt that when telling me about unsatisfactory marks, he would be doing himself favours by naming all his friends who'd scored lower than him. If he came home and announced, "Guess what I got for Maths, Mummy!" I instantly knew it was good news.

If it was bad news, he'd sometimes wait till it was almost time for bed before giving me a beseeching look and saying, "By the way, I got back my English marks today…" It is predictable behaviour but who can blame him?

Meanwhile, this was what Miss Sharifah had written in his report book:

"Noah is a fun-loving and helpful student who shows a positive attitude towards his work. He readily accepts feedback on his weaknesses and works towards improvement. This can be seen from his enthusiastic nature in class over the year. A warm, cheerful and caring boy, he takes the initiative to extend his generous assistance to his peers and this makes him a well-liked student among his classmates."

What a lovely tribute to Noah! I think it's great of her to focus on his attitude instead of on his marks. I hope he will be blessed with an equally enlightened teacher next year and be motivated to keep learning.

Ordinary Miracle

It's hard to believe that Noah has come to the end of Primary Three. Just the other day, I was walking along the footpath near our flat and had a sudden flashback of clutching Noah's chubby little hand as we traversed that route to his kindergarten together. Was that really five years ago?

I think all mothers feel a sharp pang when their youngest child grows up. Maybe that's why I'm determined to baby my little one for as long as possible, to hang on to the sweet, wonder years when the world is still waiting to be discovered.

I'm so grateful to be able to enjoy a flexible work arrangement so I can watch my kids grow up. We can't turn back time and I would probably kick myself if I'd missed out on being with them during their formative years.

Noah has matured significantly in the past year. I can see the difference even in his physical features. He has lost much of that baby-faced look as well as his baby fat, probably due to the Fitness Club regime. His obsession with Ben 10 and cartoon characters has tapered off and he has begun to steer towards his sporting abilities. He shared with me, not without some pride, that during PE, everyone wanted to be on his team. I'm not surprised as he's agile and quick, with good ball sense.

My little boy is growing up fast. But in certain aspects, he's still as child-like as ever and I hope he will maintain that innocence for as long as possible. He still climbs onto my lap and is generous with his hugs and kisses. He still holds my hand, makes silly faces and mimics silly moves. He still says the funniest, out-of-the-blue things, like in response to an insult from April, "If I'm a dust mite, you're…you're…fabric!"

Last week when I was picking Noah up from the Fitness Club, a boy dashed to the school gate, waved enthusiastically at Noah and yelled with obvious affection, "Bye, Noah!" Later I learnt that the boy was one of his classmates who was constantly getting into scrapes and having trouble making friends. I asked Noah if he was a friend and he replied, "Yes. Ming Hao told me not to be friends with him but I don't care. I'm friends with everyone."

I think it is this easy-going and gregarious nature of Noah's that enables him to accept everyone for who they are and enjoy whatever life has to offer. It is humbling that my nine-year-old should be a constant check against my own cynical attitude, and it's a real blessing for me. My wish for him is that he will never lose his innocence. At the risk of sounding like a besotted mum, I truly believe the world would be a better place if there were more Noahs in it.

The Hardest Part

This was it—the release of the PSLE results. As I drove April to school, she was impossibly jittery and nervous. "What if I don't do well?" she kept asking, fear evident on her face.

"You'll be fine!" I assured her. "Even if you don't do as well as you'd hoped, I know you studied very hard. I'm sure you'll still be able to get into a good secondary school."

The school hall was already filled when we arrived and the tension was palpable. If anxiety was inflammable, all the parents and students in that room would have spontaneously combusted. Then began the slow, torturous process of announcements by the Principal, talks by various secondary school representatives hoping to attract the best and the brightest from Somerset Primary, and finally the singing of the school song.

As I watched April move up the queue to collect her results slip, my heart was beating so fast I couldn't hear myself think. Akin to watching the climactic scene in a movie in slow motion, I saw her receive her slip from her teacher, step towards the side and open it.

Then the unthinkable happened. April's face crumpled up and she gave a little squawk, a horrible sound that I'd never heard from her before. I hurried to her side and took the results slip from her shaking hands.

T-score of 232. A*s in English and Science, an A for Chinese and a B for Maths.

232? B! That wasn't even on my radar. I was so shocked my mind couldn't process what I'd just seen. A tangled web of thoughts rushed into my head. Should I have sent her for more tuition? Did the teachers do something wrong? Maybe the results were a mistake.

I turned to April and I felt sick to my stomach. There she stood, her fists scrunched up against her eyes, sobbing uncontrollably. It was a heart-wrenching picture of a child whose hopes and dreams had been irreparably crushed.

All around her, students were either screaming with joy or pouting in disappointment. Her class did exceptionally well—a good majority of them scored at least 250. But not April. There was nothing else left to do except to take her home and lick our wounds.

I couldn't face a day at the office so I called my editor and told him I had to take urgent leave. He asked after April's results and I couldn't bring myself to tell him the exact score. I just said it wasn't good. He had two secondary school children so he understood. He tried to console me by saying the PSLE wasn't everything.

Was it not? It sure felt like it was. April had been crying non-stop and I didn't know what to say to her. I hate the PSLE. I hate that it has reduced her to a number and I hate that this number has shaken her self-esteem so badly. I hate what it has done to my beautiful daughter.

Poor Noah, clueless as usual, tried to comfort April by saying, "Miss Sharifah said if you fail, try, try again."

He was rebutted with an angry and tearful, "I'm not going to do the PSLE again, you moron!"

I was too upset myself to rebuke her for calling Noah names.

Privately, Papa told me I put too much pressure on April and made the PSLE such a big deal that she couldn't handle the fall. Why was everything my fault? I thought all I did was encourage her to achieve to the best of her ability, like every other parent did.

Later that evening when April's tears had subsided some-what, I sat with her. She turned her tear-streaked face to me and asked, "I studied so hard and I put everything else on hold. Why does it have to be like that? It's not fair."

I wanted to tell her that life sucked sometimes. That no matter how hard we wished and worked for something, it could still not materialise. That she was a bright and fan-tastic young lady, that the T-score was a mistake and didn't represent her. I wanted to say all of that and more but I couldn't because I was so overwhelmed with disappointment myself.

It's not fair.

Let It Be

I couldn't sleep for two nights. How did this one exam grow into such mammoth proportions? It didn't make any sense. At the end of the day, I know that no one single path can guarantee our success in life and certainly not one school. Many of the people I know who are doing very well today never went to the top schools. Some didn't even go to university. God knows I've failed my fair share of exams in my time.

So why did this experience make me feel like such a failure? Could it be that I'd bought into the whole academic rat race more than I had realised?

I was the one who let the scores define April, always harping on her marks, her mistakes. Here was a girl who was afraid of failure and I did nothing to help her. In fact, I reinforced it by creating an environment where she wasn't allowed to fail. This was a train wreck waiting to happen and I didn't see it coming. In the end, she was the casualty.

It's my fault.

But it's not too late. The PSLE is not all there is. She's 12. There's a whole future ahead of her and it can still be good. Just maybe not the way I have always defined 'good'.

A week after the results, I took April out for tea at her favourite café, just the two of us. Mother and daughter. We had a lovely, relaxing chat over Earl Grey and cake. We chatted, not about homework, school or exams, but about random stuff. About hairclips. About why teenagers were mad over K-pop. About which café sold the best durian cake. Stuff that seemed frivolous and insignificant, yet was somehow so important. We sat there for three hours and had the best time ever. No need to rush back for tuition, no worries about having to finish assessment books.

When was the last time I had a real heart-to-heart with my first-born? I suddenly realised that I didn't remember when she stopped wanting to hold my hand, when I last kissed her, even when I last told her I loved her. Funny how these things were so easy with Noah but so difficult with April. She just slipped away from me without me noticing and now it was so hard to break down that barrier. Thinking about it made me sad. I wish I could rewind the clock and make amends.

Halfway through tea, April looked down at her empty plate and asked in a small voice, "Do you love Noah more than me?"

"Of course not!" I said, startled. "Why would you think that?"

"Because Noah doesn't have to do well in school and you still love him. I always have to do well."

My heart shattered into a million pieces. I couldn't speak

for a few minutes. Finally I said, "I didn't mean to make you feel that way. We're here now, right? Just us."

I always thought that by telling April how smart she was, how bright she was, she would see how much I believed in her. But I never told her I loved her for who she was, not for what she could achieve. I assumed she knew. No wonder she was afraid of failure—because failing meant she wasn't good enough, she wasn't worthy of my love. I'm a journalist. I investigate to seek the truth. And I never saw the truth with my own daughter. Maybe I refused to see it because it was easier to believe that she was a perfect child with a perfect record and a perfect future.

I'm sorry for treating you like a trophy. I'm sorry for setting impossible standards that you felt you had to reach to please me. I'm sorry for forgetting that you're only 12. I'm sorry. All the things I wanted to say but couldn't.

My mind skipped to a sunlit Saturday morning a few months ago when Noah was supposed to be revising for his exams. I caught him looking out the window instead, distracted by a roving butterfly. "Noah, you're supposed to be studying!" I scolded.

He replied languidly, "I am! I'm studying what's out there."

Out of the mouth of babes…Noah, in his typical innocent manner, spoke unexpected words of wisdom. We put so much emphasis on the lessons in our books that we have forgotten about the lessons out there. Maybe Noah is the one who has gotten it right all along.

Coda

New Year's Eve

———————————

Dearest April,

Often, I marvel at how I managed to have a daughter like you. You seem to be driven by some deep, internal catalyst, such is your determination. You're mature beyond your years, thoughtful and sharp, tempered with a dollop of level-headedness. I'm constantly amazed by your discipline, sensitivity and sensibility. At the same time, your feistiness (I know I often call it pig-headedness) keeps you from being bland. I am in awe of you.

I know I push you too hard sometimes but I hope you understand it's because I believe so strongly in you. In the year ahead, I hope we can both find balance, so that the bond between us can be strengthened even further.

My wish for you this New Year is that you will delight in new experiences and not be afraid to try something different, even if you risk failure. I know that failing seems like the scariest thing in the world and people can be mean, but I promise I will be there to support you and help you up when you stumble.

I hope that you will relax more and be kinder to yourself. Do not let the expectations of others limit you or define you. Who you are is not carved in stone. You are a work in progress and it is only by embracing life and whatever is thrown at you, that you will grow in depth as a human being.

You are an incredible young lady and I love you very much.

Mummy

Dearest Noah,

Where do I begin? You are such a (big) bundle of joy. I thank God for your spontaneity, your big heart and your eagerness to please. I live for all your hugs and kisses, given with such unadulterated affection.

Sometimes I worry about your innocence, how you're so unaware of the ways of the world, and how you wear your heart on your sleeve. But I know it's this quality that makes you so genuine and lovable, and it's what draws people to you. I wouldn't trade it for the world. You keep me young because you keep me laughing! Without even trying.

I wish for you patience, something we both need. I know that for someone who lives for the moment, it is incredibly difficult for you to work towards goals that always seem so far away, and rewards that beckon only with hope, not promises.

But I pray that in this process, you will learn that diligence builds character (ugh, I know, I sound like the father in *Calvin and Hobbes*) and that you will come to understand it's the journey, not the end result, that will enrich your life.

May your generous spirit never diminish. When people

around you judge you or try to make you feel less of a person, I hope you will always be secure in the knowledge that you are a champ in every sense of the word.

You are a blessing to many and I'm truly thankful that you have been entrusted to me.

Mummy